Torah Told Different

Torah Told Different

Stories for a Pan/Poly/Post-Denominational World

ANDREW RAMER

Foreword by Tamara Cohn Eskenazi
Afterword by Sue Levi Elwell

RESOURCE *Publications* · Eugene, Oregon

TORAH TOLD DIFFERENT
Stories for a Pan/Poly/Post-Denominational World

Copyright © 2016 Andrew Ramer. All rights reserved. Except for brief quotations in critical publications or reviews, no part of this book may be reproduced in any manner without prior written permission from the publisher. Write: Permissions, Wipf and Stock Publishers, 199 W. 8th Ave., Suite 3, Eugene, OR 97401.

Resource Publications
An Imprint of Wipf and Stock Publishers
199 W. 8th Ave., Suite 3
Eugene, OR 97401

www.wipfandstock.com

PAPERBACK ISBN: 978-1-4982-8100-3
HARDCOVER ISBN: 978-1-4982-8102-7
EBOOK ISBN: 978-1-4982-8101-0

Manufactured in the U.S.A.　　　　　　　　　AUGUST 10, 2016

For my foremothers, who fed me with stories:
Nan Herman, Rose Ramer, Carla Reiss, Mina Levinson.
And Rabbi Regina Jonas, whose stories we never got to taste.

Ours is not a bloodline but a textline.
AMOS OZ & FANIA OZ-SALZBERGER, *JEWS AND WORDS*

I want an invented truth.
CLARICE LISPECTOR, *ÁGUA VIVA*

Contents

Foreword by Rabbi Tamara Cohn Eskenazi | ix

1. Twice Upon a Time | 1
2. A Torah of our Foremothers | 9
3. Verses from the Scrolls of "Zichronot" | 31
4. The Five Books of Motion | 50
5. The Secret Stories of Rosanna Ramer | 70
6. Riffing on Torah | 100

Afterword by Rabbi Sue Levi Elwell | 119
Notes | 121
Acknowledgments | 127

Foreword

THE RABBINIC SAGES OF old knew it all the time: those spaces between words and lines in the Bible are entry points to what is left unsaid and should have been said. There is black fire which are the words we actually read, and white fire that demands exploring. Rabbinic sages boldly penetrated those spaces and opened them up to hidden possibilities, awaiting discovery. Their efforts, their magical gifts of seeing the unsaid, find their legacy alive in the writings of Andrew Ramer. With the scintillating *Queering the Text*, Andrew demonstrated his unique touch of the authentic and the revolutionary. Biblical figures, lost to the casual reader, found their lives recovered and their future reclaimed. In particular, Andrew discovered, recovered, imagined the "Genizah of Dreams," the place where dreams are hidden and stored. We must remember what a Genizah is. The word carries a dual meaning, something hidden and a treasury, a place for storing what is precious. As far as scholars can tell, the Genizah had become early in history a safekeeping place for damaged holy scrolls. Being holy, they could not, should not, be discarded. Being damaged in some way, by mistakes or accidents, they could not be used. What Andrew did is create a Genizah of dreams for the readers. He gifted us with the realization that there is a place to preserve dreams that got injured, perhaps by a harsh reality not ready to accommodate them. And that these dreams are holy even when, and perhaps especially when, they don't easily find a place in the broad day light of the ordinary world. Maybe the dreams or stories that make them up need to

FOREWORD

be stored there for a time, in the library of hidden books on the 613th floor that he envisions in *Queering the Text*. But maybe they need to come out at some point and help the world become more hospitable.

Now, in *Torah Told Different*, Andrew is letting more such dreams out, and conjures up new ones, imagining the missing fourth volume to the standard tri-partite Jewish Bible we have. Some stories suffuse difficult biblical ones with sweetness that takes out the sting but preserves the power. Others make them more difficult, like "The Book of Joe," a spin on The Book of Job, that merrily moves forward as an alternate only to surprise at the end. Tough theological questions are not eschewed (see, for example, "Private Notes to God"). Then there is whimsy, interspersed throughout but sometime at the very center, married to the profound. What would YOU do if a divine messenger or God chose to appear to you while you were enjoying your bath? How do you explain to God the misery of a having a cold while making suggestions as to how God might make a better world? And what about the rabbi who, when asked about incorporating the Christmas tree into Jewish life, reaches out to the Burning Bush as an eco-kosher alternative? (as long as one follows certain rules, such as it must never have more than ten ornaments – for ten commandments and ten mystical spheres). Then there is the collection of "The Forgotten Sages," where Judith the Wise, like Rabbi Judah the Prince (presumed redactor of the *Mishnah*), collects the chain of tradition, with a twist. In this book biblical figures find themselves clothed in new daring stories. And figures who should have been there to begin with now leap forth to greet and invite us into their life; thanks to them and to Andrew, we find ourselves traversing new worlds. These are journeys not to be missed.

Rabbi Tamara Cohn Eskenazi, Ph.D.
The Effie Wise Ochs Professor of Biblical Literature and History
Hebrew Union College—Jewish Institute of Religion

1
Twice Upon a Time

THE TORAH BEGINS WITH two entirely different creation stories. The first one starts with chaos, then moves in a stately fashion toward God declaring that everything He created is, "*Tov ma'od,* very good." Conversely, the second story begins in an orderly fashion and ends with the painful expulsion of the first two human beings from the Garden of Eden.

I understand this duality. I understand Eden and the loss of Eden. When I was small, Eden was our backyard. I had my first spiritual experience there when I was five, lying on the warm grass beneath a bank of honeysuckle blossoms with my best friend Janie. Sunlight was streaming down through the branches of two large trees, a horse chestnut and a pin oak. Bees were buzzing all around us, and all at once I knew, knew in a deep embodied way, that just as the bees were dipping in and out of those sweet fragrant blossoms, over and over again—that everything that exists comes from and goes back to a Something that I did not think to call God that day.

I had my first experience of radical disconnection a year later, lying on the grass by myself, looking up at the sky, when by blinking I discovered that each of my eyes sees the sky as a slightly different color, more what I call blue with my right eye and gray with my left. Discovering that about myself thrust me out of Eden, out of unity, by shattering the innate connection I'd been living in, between words, the world, and my experience of it. "Roses are red, violets are blue." But, which red, which blue? (To this day I prefer the blue sky of my right eye and the green grass of my left.)

My Jewish education also consists of two different stories, one happening right after the other. My first Hebrew School teachers were women who told us wonderful stories, about the mythical beasts on Noah's ark and about Abraham breaking his father Terach's idols. But when we were old enough to start learning Hebrew, our teachers were suddenly all men, and I was stunned and saddened as we began to read the Torah itself—because the stories I loved weren't there, just the bare bones of them. Later I learned that those stories about stories that I first heard and fell in love with are called '*midrashim*: inquiries, investigations,' and to this day I prefer those baroque explorations to the bony versions we find in the written Torah.

From the beginning of our reading of *Genesis*, all of us, girls and boys alike, noticed who was missing from the text. We read that Adam and Eve had Cain, Abel, and then Seth, and we understood that; but when we read that Cain and Seth had children, all of us asked, "If there was no one else in the world but them and their parents—who were their wives, who were the mothers of their children?" The answer we were given by our male teacher was another midrash: "Each of them was born with a twin sister." Even as a boy I wondered, "Why didn't the Torah just say that?" And we wondered too, "Why did Jacob have so many sons and only one daughter?" But there was no midrash for that.

Twice upon a time.

We were taught that Moses received not one but two Torahs from God, one written and one oral. And when we came to the second, and different, version of the Ten Commandments, we were taught another midrash, a lovely one, that the children of Israel heard God stating both of them at the very same time; an aural version of my visual experience. Two becoming one.

> Judith the Wise said:
>
> God created through words. Therefore words tell us about the God who said: "Let there be," and there was. Therefore the most true thing is a story. And we are a people of stories.
>
> The Alexandrian Talmud, Tractate "Splendor"

Over the years my Jewish education deepened, only to be abandoned a year after my bar mitzvah. I came back to it in college, earned a degree in Jewish Studies, and then abandoned it again for decades. I never abandoned my Jewishness or my love of Jewish stories, and in those intervening years I became a storyteller myself, a writer of *midrashim,* of stories that riff on Torah. My first book, *little pictures,* published in 1987 and long out of print, is lacking in capital letters, filled with illustrations I did myself, and begins with a series of improbable creation stories that were inspired by the Torah.

By *Torah* I mean: The Five Books of Moses. I mean, by extension, the entire Hebrew Bible. By Torah I mean all of Jewish learning, sacred and secular, in every genre, from the ancient dusty past to the roiling raucous pregnant present. And ultimately by Torah I mean: the Torah of our lives.

By *Told* I mean: in words, I mean in stories, stories spoken and stories written down, as well as stories illustrated, stories danced to, and stories shared as song.

By *Different* I mean: not the same. By different I mean that I don't believe that there was a real Moses or a revelation at Sinai, but when I close my eyes I can still see where I was standing: to the southwest of the mountain, which was really just a low rise, a hillock. I can see what I was wearing, sandals and a long dusty brown robe, hanging loosely over my near-term first child. I can still see the people who were standing around me, husband, friends, family, all of us listening to a short dark hairy man with a heavy lisp talking and talking and talking as if his very life depended on it, as if ours did, and does still, to this very day.

Torah Told Different

Lydia of Tiberias said in the name of Judith the Wise:

Moses told stories from the top of a mountain. Miriam told stories while kneading bread. The Levites wrote down his words. Her attendants were too busy stoking the fires beneath the ovens to write anything down. But whenever we bless our bread and eat it, we are eating her stories.

The Damascus Talmud, Tractate "Blessings"

The rabbis of old divided their commentaries on the Torah into two categories, Halachah, which are legal ponderings, and Aggadah, which are narrative explorations. In the Orthodox world it's Halachah, Jewish law, that determines who is Jewish and what is Jewish. But I am not that kind of Jew. I'm grounded in that ancient rabbinic soil in a different way. I'm an Aggadic Jew, and you perhaps are too. It's stories, narratives, words, intonations, feelings, dreams, gossip, and even recipes that name us, label us—the passing on of recipes a fundamental form of storytelling. So imagine us sitting around a table, we Aggadic Jews who are every bit as Jewish as the Halachic ones. Imagine us sitting around a table, eating blintzes or falafels or rotis, or all three of them, as we tell each other the stories, the Torah, of our lives.

The three sections of the Hebrew Bible—Torah, Prophets, and Writings—were first spoken and then written down and edited during the period of the First and Second Temples, and canonized after the Second Temple was destroyed by the Romans in 70 CE. But I am a man who sees differently out of each eye. I am a man who lives in the world twice, and in this book you will find stories that are grounded in the texts that have come down to us through time, and you will find a second set of texts, which are grounded in alternate history.

In the real world our ancestors built two temples in Jerusalem. The first was erected by King Solomon in the mid-tenth century BCE and destroyed by the Babylonians in 587 BCE. The second was begun under the Persians in 538 BCE and destroyed by the Romans in the year 70 CE. In this book you will discover that our ancestors built a third Temple, which was begun in 363 CE under the Roman emperor Julian—who actually proposed doing so, but died too soon for it to be accomplished. You will learn too that a convocation was held in Jerusalem in the year 404, soon after that temple was completed, whose members canonized the fourth and final section of the Hebrew Bible, "Zichronot, Remembrances," under the leadership of the first woman to have been ordained a rabbi, Judith the Wise. When the Third Temple was destroyed in 537 CE, after the Final Jewish Revolt, the Romans forced the survivors of the land to completely level the city of Jerusalem and then entirely rebuild it, so that to this day no one knows where our three ancient temples stood. In 588, when a shining new city rose up from vanished hills and valleys, the Romans forced every last one of the surviving Jews into permanent exile. Luckily, the large Jewish communities in Syria, Egypt, and Italy received the fleeing refugees into their flourishing communities, their synagogues and schools, and of course into their stories.

> Salome the daughter of Leah said:
>
> To the Torah of Moses the books of the Prophets were added, by the men of the Great Assembly of Jerusalem. To the books of the Prophets the Writings were added, by the men of the Solemn Assembly of Yavneh. To the Writings the books of Remembrances were added, by the women and men of the Glorious Assembly of Jerusalem, in the days when the final temple was still standing.
>
> One God and four letters in God's holy name. One holy world, and four directions. One Holy Scripture in four sections.
>
> The Roman Talmud, Tractate "Wonder"

In the "real world" there are two Talmuds, Babylonian and Jerusalem, that were written entirely by men, in Aramaic, with a focus that is largely Halachic. But in the pages that follow you will discover a world in which there are three entirely different Talmuds that are largely Aggadic, their texts written by men and women on three different continents, in three different cities: Damascus, Alexandria, and Rome, in three different languages: Aramaic, Greek, and Latin. You won't hear the stories of how they were created, nor will you hear stories about how three different strands of Aggadic Judaism evolved from those three Talmuds. But gradually, as you read this book—you may begin to hear those stories echoing in your mind, as if I'd written them, texted them to you, as if you'd read them, scrolled through them, and lived them yourself.

All of this may sound unlikely to you, absurd, ridiculous, impossible. But we know from the archaeological record that in the third century CE a woman named Rufina of Smyrna was the head of her synagogue, as were Sophia of Gortyn and Theopempte of Myndos a century later, at the very same time that the Talmudic rabbis were recording their legal decisions—without ever mentioning those women or the others like them who had leadership roles in their communities and in their congregations. So consider the possibility that my 'imaginary' past isn't entirely made up, but summoned from beyond the grave the way that the so-called Witch of Endor brought back from the dead the prophet Samuel in the book of *Kings*.

> Julia Rachel the daughter of Miriam the Younger said:
>
> On the day that the Torah was given to our people, some of them did not accept it, nor did their descendants, as we know from history. It is therefore incumbent upon us their heirs, in every generation, to retell it in such a way that each one of us can finally receive it.
>
> The Damascus Talmud, Tractate "Questions"

In telling these stories, in the next five chapters, I will be letting you know how very much in love I am with our core texts, hoping that you will go back to them in new ways, and perhaps fall in love with them all over again, or, for the very first time.

In "A Torah of Our Foremothers" I retell stories found in the Torah through the collective voice of my own grandmothers.

"Verses from the Scrolls of Zichronot" contains selections from the imaginary fourth section of the Hebrew Bible, all of them written by women.

"The Five Books of Motion" carries our Jewish stories through history, in a series of sketches that begin with an older Moses out in the wilderness, and end in contemporary San Francisco with a little girl named Sadie who's struggling with her family's observance of Shabbat.

In "The Secret Stories of Rosanna Ramer" my imaginary grandmother tells stories that reflect upon and retell stories found in the Hebrew Bible.

The final chapter, "Riffing on Torah," take us back to the Torah itself, to the commentaries on it collected by fictional Judith the Wise's historical ancestor Judah the Prince, followed by stories about stories that carry us on through time into the future.

All of these stories emerge from the me who stood at Sinai, seven months pregnant, and the me who has long been fed by women and by women's voices: by teachers, rabbis, friends, and authors. You will find here echoes of Virginia Woolf, who played with possibilities so well in *Orlando;* Dorothy Bryant who created a compelling alternate reality in *The Kin of Ata Are Waiting for You*; and Adrienne Rich, whose *The Dream of a Common Language* and other works changed so many of our lives.

Once I sat at Rich's feet, literally, as she reclined in an orange velvet armchair in poet friend Joan Larkin's Brooklyn living room, telling stories. On another occasion, Joan dubbed me an honorary lesbian with a very large wooden spoon, as we were standing in her kitchen, a blessing that prepared me for my ordination as a *maggid*, a sacred storyteller, almost forty years later.

I had my first spiritual experience when I was five, lying under the honeysuckle blossoms with my best friend Janie. All of these stories are also illuminated by the major spiritual experience of my life, which happened to me twenty years later, when I was living in Brooklyn and God came to me, one sunny afternoon, and spoke to me while I was sitting on my bed, not as He but as She. The idea that God could be She was not something that had ever occurred to me before that afternoon, and I could say a great deal about what happened to me and also share with you the things She's said to me over the years—but that's a whole different book of stories.

Stories. The telling of stories. It's the telling of stories that connects us and keeps us alive as a people. It's Aggadah with strands of

Halachah woven through, like slow waves of chocolate in a bar of marble halvah. Wherever we've migrated to, in the years since the destruction of the Third Temple, from Shanghai to Santiago to San Francisco, we traditionally observant Aggadic Jews have brought our stories with us. Whenever we tell them, retell them, we renew our covenant with God, the earth, with each other. And doing this is an act of hope—that in telling Torah different—other things too can change. For if God made the world through words, as our tradition tells us, and then made us in Its image, we all have the power to remake our damaged world with words. Have to.

> Malkah the Elder said in the name of Judith the Wise:

When Solomon the son of David built the First Temple, the ark sat in the holy of holies, behind doors, attended by the high priest, who entered it daily. Then the Babylonians destroyed it.

When Zerubbabel the son of Shealtiel built the Second Temple under Cyrus the Persian, there was no ark in the holy of holies, no doors to it but only curtains, and only the high priest entered it, on one single day of the year. Then the Romans destroyed it.

When Abiezer the son of Gamaliel built the Third Temple under the Emperor Julian, there was no ark in the holy of holies, no doors or curtains to separate it from the holy place before it, and no one entered it, ever, not even the high priest. Then the Romans again destroyed it.

> Deborah of Barkai said in the name of Judith the Wise, her mother:

Although they were all different, all three temples were exactly the same; and should there ever be a fourth one, it too will be exactly the same.

> The Alexandrian Talmud, Tractate "Rejoicing"

2
A Torah of Our Foremothers

WE TEND TO THINK of the Torah as a primary text, perhaps *the* primary text. But even the Torah is a midrash, riffing on stories that were told before it, some remembered, most forgotten. It's a secondary text, tertiary, an anthology of stories that riff on earlier stories, about goddesses no doubt, and the enlivening spirits of the earth. Stories that go all the way back to the very first story that one human animal told another, probably a child curled up in her furry lap. "Before you born. Far. Trees we live in."

As part of that human lineage, every night when it was bedtime, after they tucked me in, my father and mother took turns reading to me, sometime from books and sometimes from the stories that Mommy wrote and Daddy illustrated on great big sheets of paper. When she was staying with us, my father's mother, Rosanna, would read to me from her favorite book (which came to me when she died)—an old crumbling edition of the sayings and stories of the great sage of the Third Temple era, Judith the Wise, whose words have been preserved in all three Talmuds.

The stories in this section are grounded in the voice of that long-dead grandmother, who I crafted from my real grandmothers. From my father's Yiddish-speaking mother Reizel, Rózia, Rose, who died when I was five, and never read to me at all, but told me all kinds of stories, sitting at her little Brooklyn kitchen table. And from my mother's mother Aniuta, Anita, Nan, who did read to me when I was a boy. We called her Nanny, her apartment was filled with art done by women, she only listened to music from Russian composers, and—Nanny didn't believe in children's books. Instead, she read to me from whatever she happened to be reading herself, Dickens, Zola, Twain, de Maupassant, and Nanny also spun for me endless tales about her childhood in Russia, stories that I still remember, although she died when I was in fifth grade.

My stories are also shaped by Carla, a refugee from Hitler's Europe who adopted me as her grandson, and who wandered in and out of English, Italian, Hungarian, and German to express herself, in delicious spiraling stories, stories so long that it seemed as if she would never come back to where she started, or tie up all the loose ends—until she did, always did, her sparkling eyes enlarged like an owl's behind the thick pale-blue tinted lenses of her glasses.

Another voice that shaped these stories belongs to Nanny's youngest sister, Manya, Mina. The two sisters didn't speak to each for years, Nanny called Mina a witch, and the first time I met Mina was when we were sitting *shiva* for Nanny—the week of formal mourning—after she died. Slowly, a visit at a time (being a man in need of one, after Grandma Carla died) Aunt Mina became my surrogate grandmother. For six years as she was moving toward the end of her life, I went to see her every Wednesday, to shop for her and keep her company. Her two great joys denied her by old age—wandering Manhattan from gallery to art gallery in high heels, and coming home to read, voraciously—Mina would sit in bed propped up on pillows, calling my grandmother a liar, and then telling me the exact same stories that Nanny had told me, claiming they happened to her instead.

As for me, I like to tell the same old stories . . . differently.

GENESIS CHAPTER ZERO

Chapter 0, verse 1

Before God began to create anything, before there was heaven or earth, night or day, good or bad, in or out, up or down, God said, "I must create Myself."

Chapter 0, verse 2

And in the vast limitless nothingness of Its allness, with no borders or boundaries, no direction and no distinctions in Its infinite eternal Self, God said, "Let there be Me."

Chapter 0, verse 3

Then God stirred and stretched and shrank and strived and sighed and surged until She became who He is. And Her isness is who He always was and always will be, in the midst of Her sacred unfolding. And God called Himself Whole and saw everything that was possible from Her radiant wholeness. And there was Someone, and there was somewhen; and from that somewhen, God was finally ready to begin to create a somewhere.

THE TREE OF WHOLENESS

After God had created the world, She sat back and rested for a while, then wandered around to look things over. The world She'd made was lovely, She decided. It revolved so elegantly around its shining star, and its seasons came and went so nicely, over and over again. The landscapes were beautiful, She decided, but something was missing. Then it occurred to her, and She pulled a small clay ocarina out of Her purse and started to play, enticing up from the ground soft sweet grasses and a whole array of flowers, flowers which began in monochrome and ended up a shimmering riot of thousands of different shapes and exploding colors, as Her sweet little tune grew more and more intricate.

Pleased with the flowers, She went on playing, and bushes rose up from the ground, then trees. Turning in circles, facing every direction, dancing in the center of the world, Her melody deepened as small and then larger and larger animals began to appear all around Her, slithering, crawling, jumping, scampering, running, racing, and flying. "Yes, this feels right," She said, smiling, admiring Her handiwork.

Yes, everything on Her world was flourishing and beautiful. But something was still missing, She decided, a little something that She couldn't put her finger on. And then it occurred to her: "Something to shake things up!" So She put Her ocarina away, closed Her eyes, took a deep in-breath, exhaled slowly—and there she was, standing right in front of Her: a person.

"Your name is Ahuvah, my dear, because you are so lovely this morning, my beloved child," God said to her. Ahuvah looked slightly embarrassed, confused, even lost perhaps, although she was smiling. So God made her a beautiful garden to dwell in, and God turned to Ahuvah and said, 'Dear, you are free to eat all of the fruits that grow in this garden. They are as tasty to the palate as they are beautiful to the eye, if I do say so myself. And be particularly certain that you eat the berries on those bushes over there, the pretty blues ones with the little crowns on top. Those berries are chock full of nutrients that will make the neurons in your brain go wild with new synapses."

So Ahuvah ate. And everything that she ate, her chin dripping with sweet nectar, she found to be just as delicious as God had assured her that it would be.

Then God said, 'You know, having been alone myself for more than a zillion years," (She said zillion for it seemed wiser to name a huge number than to try and explain eternity) "I'm really not sure that it's such a good idea for you to be alone." Then God told the woman a very long story, about all the steps in the creation of the world, going from pure nothing to manifest somewhereness.

And the story put Ahuvah to sleep, just as God hoped it would. And God said:

> "It is not good for a woman to be alone. After all, I am alone, and one alone is enough."

While Ahuvah slept, God put life in her womb and the woman's body began to swell. When she woke Ahuvah was amazed and said to God, "Now I have become like You and like the earth itself." God said "Exactly. For you are my beloved child, my human mirror. And you, a woman, will be the singular parent of every human being who will ever live." And in nine months time Ahuvah brought forth from her body four children, because four is a holy number. A man child. A woman child. A child who at different times of the day was neither a woman nor a man, and a child who in certain lights was both of them.

The children grew and multiplied, and they did the sorts of things that children do today. And God could see the way that things were going, and She was pleased—for this was exactly what She'd wanted—something to shake things up a little bit. But, aware of the risk of them going too far—in a far corner of the garden, God planted a tiny little tree, the Tree of Wholeness, in celebration of Ahuvah, Her final creation, and of her children and their children down through time. The tree grew up so slowly that even though it was planted for them, the first woman and her children never noticed it as they wandered about, never saw even a tiny single little shoot spring up from that tree into the blue blue aching sky.

"Yes, this tree that I planted will bear flowers and fruits, slowly, in its corner of the garden, taking thousands and thousands of years to mature. It will scatter its seeds slowly, very slowly, by wind, all across the world. And those seeds will burrow in and take root, slowly. And then slowly again, taking thousands and thousands of years, new saplings will grow up from those scattered seeds, slowly waiting for the right time to begin to bear fruit to be eaten by My wise and foolish children, who will have learned much I am certain, and done much, and will only need then to remember how to be whole again. Wholeness being the gift of the fruit of this quiet little hidden tree. "

THE FIRST REALLY BIG PROJECT

The first people, even way back then, did what people still do—they reproduced. Soon there were more and more people, all of them doing what people like to do: cause trouble. God sat back, watching. The angels, flittering in the background, said to each other—"Bad idea, to give them so much freedom."

All of the people were living in the same place, and it was getting crowded. Eventually a man among them came up with the idea of building a tower for all of them to live in, a tower so high that they could get to heaven without having to die first. Everyone thought that was a great idea, and they set to work building it, on the outskirts of their city.

There was a woman in that first city in the world whose name was Naamah, and Naamah thought that building such a tower was a terrible idea. "What we should be doing," she announced in the marketplace, "is to build a great big dance floor where we can all come together to celebrate being in the world. A place where we can dance and sing and tell our stories." But no one listened to her, and the few people who did ended up laughing at her. "Imagine, a dance floor, when we could build a tower up to heaven!"

The tower would take many years to build, and would involve the labor of all of the people. As it grew skyward the tower was a wondrous thing to behold, tall and made of shiny stones that sparkled in the sunlight. When it was exactly half done, the people decided to hold a big celebration. Everyone came, all dressed in their finery. They climbed the broad stone steps that led to the entrance of the tower, and everyone thought: "We are the most amazing people who ever lived!"

It was late in the afternoon of the day of celebration, a beautiful warm day. Some people were partying on the lower floors while others were wandering up its many inner stairs to explore it—when all at once, because they weren't strong enough—all at once, with a sound like thunder multiplied by ten thousand—all at once the walls of the tower shattered and the great tower collapsed, killing most of the celebrants and destroying much of the sprawling city that surrounded it.

Looking down the angels said, "This comes as no surprise."

Looking down God thought, "Maybe making people wasn't such a good idea."

Although he was inebriated, the man who came up with the idea for the tower survived. He insisted that his idea was a sound one, but that the people working on it had not followed his instructions. Few of them remained to tell their side of the story, and the ones who did, buried their dead, left that place of loss and pain, and wandered off to start new towns and cities.

As for Naamah, the woman who wanted everyone to build a dance floor, she survived too. And she looked at the ruins, the remains of streets, rubble-filled, abandoned, and she said to herself—"What a tragedy." Then she set up a tent on the edge of the ruins, and every day she climbed the piles of stones, she wandered the rubble, searching

Day after day, year after year, she sorted through the ruins, carting out undamaged stones and arranging them on the edge of what had been the city. And gradually, from out of the rubble, she lay out a very large flat stone circle, a gigantic non-reflecting mirror for the moon and for the sun and the stars. From time to time over the years a caravan would wander by the remains of the first city and its fallen tower. And they would see, among the ruins, a very old old woman carting stones and arranging them into what looked like a dance floor. Some had their musical instruments with them, flutes and drums, and they would join the old woman to make music and dance. But most of the time the people in the caravans who passed, if they stopped at all, would look at the old woman and laugh, laugh at her, and travel on.

Some years later, when Naamah knew that her days were at an end, she curled up in a crack in a pile of rubble and died there. And in time, as the remains of the tower continued to crumble, her grave and her dance floor were covered over and forgotten. The angels said, "Another bad idea."

And God, She sighed.

EMZARAH'S ARK

The people in the world got worse and worse. They damaged the soil, they harmed the plants and animals, and they so ruined the weather that the seasons were thrown off and it began to rain—all the time. Someone invented the umbrella, and became the world's first millionaire. Others grew rich making raincoats and waterproof boots. And everyone went about their business as if nothing was the matter, except for a single man who decided to build a boat, a boat just big enough for his family to fit in, his family and a few of all the animals in the world. Which they did.

Every morning when he got up, listening to the rains that battered above them and the waves that crashed beneath them, Noah would stretch and look around and smile. "I am a clever man," he would say to himself, "and I am here, alive and well, with my dear wife Emzarah and our wonderful boys and their wonderful wives." Then he would thank God for saving them, and whistling, he would get up and join Emzarah in the small galley where she was already preparing their morning meal.

Every morning Emzarah and Noah's sons Shem, Ham, and Japheth, would wake and stretch, and listening to the battering rain and the crashing waves, think, "We are such lucky boys, to still be alive, because we are the clever sons of a clever father." And their wives, Sedek, Neelat, and Adat, snuggled close to their husbands for warmth in their narrow stalls, would wake and think, listening to the battering rains and the crashing waves, "We are such lucky girls, to still be alive, because we married the clever sons of a clever man."

And the sons and their wives would join Emzarah and Noah for their morning meal, of stored grains and milk and eggs taken from the animals on board. And when they were done they would thank the One who had preserved them, and with Noah whistling, they would all go off to do their morning tasks, of feeding the animals and cleaning up after them, except for Adat, who was often seasick—or pretending to be, her sisters-in-law suspected.

Every morning after breakfast, Emzarah would clean up and then she would wander from top to bottom of the ark, checking on the animals, petting, grooming, and comforting them, trapped in their tiny stalls, as the ship surged and tilted, all of them tormented by the battering rain above and the crashing waves beneath their fragile home.

When the rains stopped and the waters receded, the ark finally came to rest on the top of a windswept mountain, and the eight of them emerged into the blinding light of a cloudless day, leading the animals out, two by two, who dashed, ran, raced, soared, slinked, slithered, ambled, and crawled off to find new homes. And Noah and his sons and their wives descended from that lonely mountain, and thanked God for their salvation, and offered sacrifices. And Emzarah, looking around them, at the twisted trees, the mangled bodies of animals and humans scattered everywhere in the mud, thought to herself, "I knew that no good would come from being trapped in that awful floating prison. No, I wish that I had died, with my parents and my sisters and their husbands and all of their children."

THE LIFE OF SARAH

Sarah stood on a rise, looking down at the circle of tents, all bathed in a soft warm light. She was coming from her morning prayers beneath the sacred tree, on her way back to build a fire and prepare the morning meal. She'd stood on this spot many times before. But something was different this morning, a clarity in the air, a stillness over the camp. And her heart was flooded with joy for this life of hers, so far from her birthplace, so different from any life she'd imagined when she was younger.

Below, her two eldest daughters emerged from their tent, fifteen year old Atirat and thirteen year old Yonat, both of them born in Haran. They didn't see her because they too were caught up in the magic of the morning. And then her third daughter Kalilah emerged, age eleven, who'd been born in Canaan a year after they arrived. Kalilah paused, looked around, and the splendor of the morning grabbed her in its embrace. Turning back to the tent, Sarah could hear Kalilah call through the flap to her youngest sister, "Quick. The sun." Eight year old Davah stepped out, just in time to see the fiery orb rise up above the hills, radiant and golden.

For a moment Sarah and her daughters were woven together in a web of shimmering light. Then Abraham emerged from her tent, holding three year old Isaac in his arms, the son of her flesh that Abraham had so longed for. Standing there, it seemed as if her husband and children were inside her. Sun, sky, land, all that too was inside her. Then Isaac turned in his father's arms and saw Sarah standing above them. "Imah, Imah!" he called out, his little voice breaking the stillness, sending the light flashing out in a thousand directions. "Yes, this is my life," Sarah said to herself, waving down at him. "And in spite of everything, our coming and going, Lot and that tragedy, and then the nightmare with Hagar and Ishmael—it's a good life." Laughing, she gathered up the corners of her robe and headed down to join her family.

SARAH'S TEST

One day, while she was on her knees in front of her tent, kneading dough for the day's bread, God called out to her, "Sarah, Sarah." Pausing for a moment, she turned to God and said, "Here I am." God spoke to Sarah and said, "There's a well at the edge of the village. I would like you to take your daughter Davah, who you love, and throw her into the water, as an offering to Me, for I am the Wellspring of Life." Wiping the flour off her hands, Sarah turned to God and said, "Are You out of Your mind? That's the best well in the area. There's no way I'm going to pollute it by throwing my daughter in, or anything else, for that matter. Not a turtledove or even a tiny little mouse. And more to the point, I know that You can create anything You want, just by speaking it into existence.

But I was pregnant for nine long months with that wonderful girl, and there's no way I'm going to end her life, just to satisfy You."

That was exactly the answer God was hoping for. Delighted, God told Sarah that it was only a test. "Well," responded Sarah, "You're going to have to work hard to earn my trust again," and then she turned back to her bread. Which is why God was so disappointed in Abraham, who was tested in the same way soon after. That time God had to send an angel to stop Abraham from killing dear young Isaac, and trap a ram in a bush for him to offer up instead. (You can imagine what the dispatched angel thought.)

SARAH'S DEATH

After Abraham untied his beloved son and slaughtered that ram in his place, Isaac turned to him, enraged, and said, "I don't want to ever lay eyes on you again. Tell Imah I'm going to Beer-lahai-roi to live with Ishmael and Hagar," and he took off from that mountain by himself, heading south.

When Abraham returned and delivered Isaac's message, Sarah shouted at him, "You've dragged me from the Euphrates to the Nile. We wandered in crazy circles for years. You traded me off to other men. But this is the straw that broke the camel's back." (Camels had only recently been domesticated and Sarah was actually the very first person to ever say those words.) She packed up her tent and moved to a village later called Kiriat-arba, Town of the Four, after her four daughters and their families, who all went with her.

Many years later, when she was 127, Sarah took to her bed for the very last time. Her daughters sat with her, Atirat rubbing her head, Yonat her feet, Kalilah singing to her, and Davah tenderly holding her wizened hand. Nearly blind, she turned to look at each one of them for the last time and said, "In spite of everything, I've had a good life. But I leave this world with two regrets." Her daughters leaned closer, so that they could hear her whisper, as she told them about the test that God had given her, which she'd never spoken of before, not to anyone. "If only I'd told Abraham. Perhaps he wouldn't have taken your brother off that way." Atirat leaned over and kissed her mother's cheek. "Imah, Isaac is fine. He's happy and well. There's nothing for you to feel badly about." Sarah sighed. "But, what I did to Hagar and Ishmael. It was terrible. Promise me that you will go to them and beg their forgiveness." They promised that they would. "And when I am gone, send for Abraham. I don't regret leaving him, but tell him that he was the only man I ever really loved."

With that, Sarah sank back into her bed of pleasure and pain, of nightmare and rest, of opening and closing. "Yes, I've had a good life," she said again, then shut her large dark eyes and breathed her last. It was her daughters' wailing that alerted the rest of the camp to their matriarch's passing. They washed her body and rubbed it with scented oils. They wrapped her in the colorful shawls she loved to wear and sat with her till Abraham came three days later, to eulogize Sarah and bewail her, just as the Torah says.

WITH A STRANGER

Twenty years had gone by since Jacob had last seen his older twin brother Esau, whose birthright he had tricked away from him, stolen away from him. Jacob had fled, fearing for his life, seeking shelter with his father's kin far to the north. There he'd married and taken concubines and fathered a host of daughters and sons, with Leah and Rachel, Bilhah and Zilpah. During those years away, Jacob prospered. And finally he was ready to go back to Canaan, to face his wronged brother and try to make peace with him.

It was a long long journey, with women and children and servants, most of them on foot, and with flocks behind them, all of them moving slowly, south and west toward Canaan. When they were nearly back, Jacob sent messengers ahead to find Esau his brother and tell him of his return. Fearing vengeance, terrified for the life of his family, Jacob prepared numerous gifts for his much-wronged brother.

The night before the feared reunion, Jacob could not sleep. He tossed and turned and in the middle of the night, wide awake, he thought he heard (or was he imagining it?) the faint sound of drumming in the distance. Slipping into his sandals, a full moon lighting his path, Jacob crossed a narrow stream and made his way toward the sound. Louder it grew as he advanced, till ahead, in a clearing of trees, he saw a lone man dancing around a flickering fire, two drummers seated on the ground carrying the rhythm that he danced to. At first, in the firelight, the man looked like an angel, but as Jacob approached, a tall dark very human man turned to face him, and offered an outstretched hand, which Jacob took. And there, around that fire, to the beat of those drums, the two of them danced, and danced, and danced, till the first light of morning whispered itself up and over the craggy pink horizon.

Now Esau that night had not been able to sleep either. His body was too filled with anger and thoughts of revenge. But instead of tossing and turning he woke two of his sons-in-law and asked them to drum for him, to drum him toward morning, hoping to dance out all the rage that was surging through his body. And when Esau saw a stranger coming toward him through the trees—he froze. For he knew as soon as he saw that man enter the clearing, his face clear in the light of the full moon—he knew that the stranger was Jacob his twin. And he knew too that in spite of everything that had happened to Jacob in the intervening years, that he still could not see what was before him, that he had not recognized him, his only brother, who he had so wronged those twenty years before. But instead of bitterness or anger, Esau was filled with pity for his twin. He moved toward Jacob, offered a hand to him, which his anxious heartless unseeing brother took. And so the twin sons of Rebecca and Isaac danced around that fire all through the night, till the first light of a new morning softly whispered itself up and over the bright shining treetops.

Then the drummers stopped drumming, got up and left the clearing. And Jacob turned to the stranger and said, "What is your name?" The strange man replied to him, "You must not ask my name." To which Jacob said, "In that case, will you bless me?" And Esau placed his hands upon Jacob's head and said, "We are all created in the image of God, and we have danced for Him all through the night. So from this moment on your name shall be Mechol'el, the man who dances with El and is forgiven by Him." And Esau bowed to his stunned, recognized but unrecognizing brother, both of them profoundly changed by their encounter. Then Esau turned and left the clearing, as Jacob bowed and turned the other way, returning to his encampment.

There Jacob roused his family, his servants, readied them for their departure, and they all made their slow slow way toward the designated place of meeting. And at the height of day, two men slowly walked toward each other, Jacob afraid, Esau amused, waiting for Jacob to look at him, to notice. Thirty feet apart, seeing but not seeing, Jacob continued to walk, and Esau stopped, and waited. Twenty feet apart. Fifteen. And then, in the bright light of day, ten feet away from each other, Jacob stopped and finally saw the stranger standing before him, and realized who he was. And Esau called out to his brother Jacob by his new name, saying, "Mechol'el, my brother, welcome home!" Then the two, with hair and beards streaked gray, wrinkled, older, both of them toughened by life, and softened by it in such different ways—the two of them, twins, fell into each others arms, weeping.

That night, around a dancing fire, surrounded by their all of their many wives and children, to the resounding beat of four seated drummers, the two of them, twins, and all of their family, danced till the moon set, till the stars had completed their nightly orbits, till the sun itself rose up again, a single bright face, shining and blessing them. And they set up their camps side by side, living that way till the end of their lives. And each month, on the night of the full moon, the two of them, the two brothers, the twin sons of Rebecca and Isaac, would dance together beneath the circling stars. And so their children did, and their children, and then their children, down through time. And so it is that we dance, that we dance, that we dance together to this day, when the moon is full in the star-strewn sky. For we are all Mechol'el, the people who dance with God.

THE BLESSINGS OF THE MOTHERS

As Rachel lay dying, after giving birth to the child she named Ben-Oni, "Son of My Sorrow," Deborah her childhood nurse called into her tent her four daughters, Maacah, Rabat, and the twins Tovah and Zillah. They knelt by their mother's bed and she weakly smiled up at them, weary, damp, afraid. They took her hands, they stroked her face, they cradled her in their arms. And she reached out to them with her last whispered words. To Maacah she said, "You were my firstborn. You have helped care for your brother Joseph and your sisters. Now help to care for this little one. You are my right hand." There were tears in her eyes, in all their eyes, as she turned Rabat and said to her, "You are the one everyone turns to in times of danger. Carry always this strength for our people. They will need it." Then, she turned to the twins, and placed her hands, already turning ashen gray, upon their heads. "Together you came into the world. May the love that binds you now always bind you. May the secret wisdom that binds you be passed on to all who follow." With that, she sank back into her bed of birth and death, of opening and closing. She sighed, shut her large dark eyes, and breathed her last. It was her daughters' sobbing that alerted their brother Joseph, their father, aunts, and the rest of their clan. And they buried Rachel beside the road, near where they had set up camp.

Bilhah was working in the fields when a swift pain shot through her heart and she tumbled to the ground, in the midst of the barley. Her daughter Shira, who was working with her, dropped her sickle and ran like a mountain goat, smashing golden stalks beneath her bare feet. There was a look of horror on her mother's face, as Shira sank to the dry earth beside her. Grabbing her hand she called to her, "Mother! Mother!" but she was vanishing, right before Shira's eyes, as if she were sinking down in a well, the light in her eyes disappearing as she fell. "Mother!" Shira cried out again. For an instant, Bilhah was back, back behind her eyes. She looked up at her panting daughter, and smiled. All the fear washed from her face. Then she was gone. But for the rest of her life, Shira could close her eyes and see that last smile, that luminous blessing of wordless joy which said, "You are here. You are here beside me, my beloved child. And now everything is all right." And she was buried near Bethel, beside the field in which she perished, by her daughters and sons, by her husband and all of his other wives and children.

Everyone was surprised when Bilhah died, for she had never been sick a day in her life. But her sister Zilpah had one illness after another, and everyone was surprised that she lived on and on and on. Zilpah's daughters Gal, Hadar, and Yael all took care of her, washing her, grooming her, rubbing oils and unguents into her bedsores, carrying her out into the sun to warm her bones. When Gal and Hadar married, their youngest sister Yael remained with Zilpah. She slept on a pallet in her mother's tent, and day and night she was there to attend her. Often, in her musings, Yael would think about her mother's death, and wonder what her life would be like when she was gone. And so it was, on her bed of pain, that Zilpah turned to her daughter as she breathed her last, and said to her, "You were so wonderful to me. And now it is time to live your own life." They buried Zilpah at Bethel, next to her sister. And Yael, the most devoted of daughters, mourned and wept and lived out the rest of her life, never marrying, never a mother herself, always caring for others.

"The first thing you notice about Mother," Leah's children said, "is her weak eyes, and the one thing you can't forget is her temper." She was proud of her six sons, but always critical of them, and relied upon her daughters Rizpah and Dinah, but never stopped complaining. Eventually the boys, as they grew into men, simply avoided her, but her girls could not do the same as they became women. They were forced to take care of her, for which she ought to have been grateful. But she never forgave Rizpah for wandering off to the nearby Canaanite village, all those years before, to meet the girls who lived there, and would peer at her with a look that said, "Rizpah, it's your fault that your sister was raped." And the way that Leah turned away from Dinah, as if she were soiled, and then later, when she had moved into her niece Serach's tent, as if she were, not happy in love, but a failure, felt like being slapped to Dinah, over and over again. "No wonder Daddy favored Aunt Rachel," her children whispered to each other. On her deathbed, with Rizpah on one side and Dinah on the other, panting, she said to them between desperate breaths. "I know I wasn't the best of mothers to you, but . . ." Then she sighed, exhaled, breathed her last, her family buried her in the family tomb in Hebron, and for the rest of their lives, Rizpah and Dinah, even on their own deathbeds in Egypt, wondered what Leah would have said to them, how she might have finally blessed them.

Jacob's first four wives, married in the land of his ancestors in the north, all died before him and were buried in the land of Canaan. It was only Adah, his fifth wife, the wife of his old age, who brought him comfort and joy again. It was only Adah, Adah of the sweet voice who moved like a gazelle, who went down with her husband and his family, down into Egypt.

Some said her family married her off to him for his money. They did. She had no say in the matter. But in time she came to love him, and she was with Jacob when he died, and she sat in mourning with his body for a week, and continued to mourn him for the seventy days that it took for his body to be mummified, in the way of the Egyptians. From that point on she lived a quiet life, in the Delta city where Jacob's family settled, she and her young daughters, Gali, Anat, and Batshua. And when her daughters came of age she said to them, "Your father I loved, but his kinsmen are troubled. You are all wise, kind, and good, and deserve better than marrying amongst them. Please promise me that you will take for yourselves husbands from among the Egyptians, husbands who can dance, not fight, husbands who can sing not shout," and they did. When Adah was dying she said to them, "Someday, our people will leave Egypt, but please stay here. And someday the descendants of Jacob will come back to Egypt, many many years from now. They will live in the Delta again, in better times. And when they do, your descendants will find them, and teach them again all that you know of our people, all the stories and dances and songs that they have forgotten." And that is exactly what happened.

NACHSHON'S STORY

I always felt different, being one of Ahuvah's children who wanders between genders, and because of that I did my very best as a child to remain unnoticed, unseen. And I know that if God hadn't softened Pharaoh's heart we would still be slaves to this very day—and I would still be living on the fringes.

Now Pharaoh was quite a handsome man, but so stubborn in his opinion of his opinions that each time God softened his heart—he hardened it again. And I know what people say about Moses, that he saved us—but without his wise and well-organized sister Miriam we might all be free, but we would still be living in Egypt, subject to Pharaoh's changing moods. And I know what people say about me, that the sea did not part until I'd stepped into its roiling waters, proving my great faith in God and in God's promise to redeem us and save us, all of us and our descendants.

Till the end of their lives Miriam always and Moses occasionally praised me, and our people continue to praise me. Over the years I've grown used to it, even come to appreciate it, a little bit. But now, now that I am old and waiting for death to claim me as it didn't do that day, now for the first time I can tell the truth, tell you what I've never told anyone before—because I was always too ashamed.

The day was hot. I remember that. The sky was cloudless. I remember that too. And fast approaching, raising up a huge cloud of dust, were Pharaoh and his soldiers coming after us, their escaped slaves. In front of us, were those great waves, crashing. We were terrified, all of us, to be trapped like that, between one kind of death and another. Between being massacred, or drowning. And we were enraged at Moses, for leading us out like that, and angry at God, for leading us out to certain death.

Hot as the day was, I was shivering, cold, with goose bumps up and down my arms and legs. Clutching the little cloth-wrapped bundle in which I'd tied up my very few possessions, I remember how I looked ahead at the great endless waters, looked behind me at the approaching clouds of Pharaoh's army. And I knew that I, that we, would all soon die, beneath the waves or by soldiers' arrows. And I stood right at the water's edge, immobile, unable to move. And while it's true that I was the very first of our people to step into those icy waters, it was not because I was brave, not because I was desperate, not because I was a total fool, and not because I ever thought that I could part them. No, I stepped into the surging waters because someone standing right behind me pushed me. Perhaps an angel, but I doubt it. Whoever it was, the moment I stepped in, as you know, the waters miraculously parted. And this is my legacy, which I can tell you now, as I lie on my deathbed, taking my final labored breaths. And this is what I've learned, after all these years of being secretly ashamed of the truth. That pushed or not, I was indeed the first to step into the waters. And pushed, as we all are, is sometimes the way the world changes.

THE BOOK OF MIRIAM

The words of Miriam the daughter of Jochebed, after the coming out from Egypt:

In the wilderness of Sinai, in the night, a vision came to me, as I lay awake, looking out of my tent, in the hour when the last watch circles the camp. In the light of a full moon the mountain beneath which we were camped was bathed in silver light. And in my vision there came down upon it great rivers of light from the heavens, light of liquid silver. And the water came rushing down the mountain in runnels, like after a spring rain. And there was a wadi where this water gathered, pooling till it resembled a reflecting mirror made of polished silver.

And in the light there was a voice, the voice of a woman, and she spoke to me saying, "Miriam, Miriam, come down to these waters." So I left my tent in the night and I walked toward the voice. And I came to that wadi, and there, before me, was the vision of a bubbling spring. And above the spring was a light, and a light within the light, as the purest fire within a flame. And in the midst of the fire was the form of a woman, dark with long streaming silver hair, and She said to me, "Kneel Miriam and drink, for this is the water of life." So I knelt and I drank, and the sweetness of water was like the sweetest of Egyptian palm wine. And when I raised my eyes to see Her, she said to me, "I am the Tree of Life, I am the Fountain of Life, I am the Mother of Life."

Then the vision drew itself up into the silver light. And for a moment that silver light filled the heavens until night was brighter than day. And then the light faded, and in the paler light of a moon grown full I saw before me, where there had been no water before—a tiny spring bubbling up from the earth, a spring rippling out into a silver shining pool. And I drank from it, and I sat beside it, till the vision faded. When the sun rose up I walked back to our camp, and I showed it to my brothers and to all of our people. And we drank, and we filled our jugs from it. And when we left that encampment, the spring disappeared. And when we stopped and set up camp again, our tents bursting up from the land like wildflowers, again that spring appeared for us, and it followed us everywhere we wandered from that time on.

Two years later there came to me another vision, in the wilderness of Zin. Again I saw a great light, and in the light I saw a throne, and on that throne was seated the Mother of Life. And She said to me, "Miriam, tell the women of your people that what your brother was taught in words I teach to you now in song. And I saw myself in Her lap, small as an infant. And she rocked me and held me and sang to me a wordless song." Teach this song to the women of your people, that they may sing it to their children. It is the song that Naamah sang, all those years ago, now passed on to you." And I said to Her, "Who am I, without husband or children, to be such a teacher?" And She laughed and said, "Miriam, Miriam. Am I not the same? Single, alone, and yet the Mother of all that is. And so you are, a tender mother to your people." So I learned the song of Naamah and I taught it to the people. "For in this song," She said, "is all the truth of what you need to know, how to love, how to cherish, how to care for each other in peace."

In my fifty-third year, at our encampment in Kadesh, again a vision came to me, as I was lying in my tent, alone on my pallet.

Suddenly the voice of the Mother of Life came to me, and again I saw Her seated on a throne, surrounded by angels. And she said to me, "Miriam, Miriam, come closer." And I did. And she said to me then, "My daughter, at the end of this year, surely you will die. And when you die the spring that has followed your people will die with you. But the wordless song of Naamah that you taught them will continue to nourish their thirsty souls. Your people will pass it down, from mother to child, generation after generation. And they will dance to it, as danced before Me your ancestor Jacob and his brother Esau. But over time the song will fade, and when it fades, your people will have to dig deeper in their souls than before to find its sweetness. And some of them will find it, and others won't."

Again I heard the song, and again I saw myself as I was when I was still a young woman, dancing to that song in the midst of the people. And I sang, and I danced, and I was glad. Then the vision faded, and I was alone again on my pallet. I called for the young women who attend me. And they washed me and they dressed and they supported me, one on each side. And in front of the Tent of Meeting I taught again that song to all the people, knowing that in so teaching it I was preparing them for my death, by giving up to them my legacy while still I breathed.

AND THEY WORSHIPPED

It was near to the end of the year when the people came to an open plain in the wilderness, an open plain with an oasis beside it. They rested there, eating from the land, drinking from its magical healing waters. And when they were rested Miriam said to them, "In ten days time we shall have a convocation, to celebrate our survival and prepare ourselves for our continuing journey. For on his deathbed our ancestor Jacob asked us to go back to Canaan to bury him there, and to then continue our wanderings through the world, as our people have done from the time of Sarah and Abraham. But we did not do that. We stayed in Egypt. And now," Miriam reminded them, "now we can return to our right path, now that we have lived as free people, no longer afraid."

"Gather stones together," Miriam said, "and make from them a giant ring, a circle, a hoop, an enclosure, all around the rise in the center of our camp." And the people did just that. When they were done, they took out their drums and their timbrels, and day and night for the next eight days, the people danced there, and they danced there, and they danced. To honor Naamah, whose song they danced to. They danced to honor Jacob who had danced all night with an angel. They danced to honor him, they danced to the Mother, their God, they danced and they sang and they rejoiced, all the women and men and their children. And their dance was a covenant that they made with each other, for all of time. And there Miriam blessed them, and they danced around her to the song that she had taught them, danced all through the night. And it was there that they buried her, a day later, for she died as the sun rose high above the dancers. She died smiling, surrounded by all of them.

3
Verses from the Scrolls of "Zichronot"

"Zichronot," the forth and final section of the *Tankaz*, the Hebrew Bible, is usually translated as "Remembrances," or simply as "Memories." After the opening book, *Judith*, we find the scrolls of *Tobit, Maccabees, The Wisdom of Solomon, The Wisdom of Ben Sirach, The Visions of Rachel the Dreamer, The Testament of Queen Helena, The Psalms of the Singers of the House of God, The Visions of the Pious Sages,* and *The Chronicles of Miriam the Just.*

The books in "Zichronot" were canonized in the early years of the Third Temple by the women and men of the Glorious Assembly of Jerusalem, under the direction of Judith the Wise, and they reflect the joyous triumphalism of that era. The elders who added these ten books to the three sections of the Bible compiled after the destruction of the Second Temple had before them hundreds of texts, some of which still exist outside the *Tankaz*. Rabbi Alberta Levy-Chan, in her study, *The Closing of the Hebrew Bible*, reminds us of the principles the sages followed. They rejected popular books like *Enoch, Baruch, Esdras,* and *Jubilees*, which parallel material found in the already canonized sections of the Bible. To be included, the sages agreed, a book must have been written in Hebrew, before the destruction of the Second Temple, with occasional words or verses in Aramaic, Greek, or Latin, and it had to be widely read, studied, and quoted, by rabbis, sages, and scholars in established Jewish communities around the world.

Including *Tobit,* a work of fiction, allowed them to step beyond the notion of Divine Revelation as the signature of a sacred book, and also validated the adoration of angels which was popular in their time. Their inclusion of the book *Maccabees* sanctified the observance of the festival of Hanukkah. But by beginning "Zichronot" with *Judith,* a book about a woman warrior, the sages were making a powerful statement—that the days of patriarchal dominance enshrined in the first three sections of the Bible were over.

We see their radical genius at work in the inclusion of Rachel the Dreamer's dreams about a female God. Levy-Chan charts Her evolution from Asherah, God's banished First Temple consort, to her Second Temple resurrection as *Chochmah* or Wisdom, and Her early rabbinic reincarnation as *Shechinah,* God's indwelling female presence in His world. But in Rachel's dreams we encounter God as female, with no explanation or justification, as if the authors of the Torah had seen God that way too, and just forgot to mention it.

This short book, the final volume admitted to the canon, was hotly debated for months. We read in the Roman Talmud that when the sages announced that this book would not be included in the Bible, during the week-long Shavuot celebration they had instituted, the crowd in the inner courtyard of the temple shouted in one voice—"If Rachel's dreams are not added, we will stop bringing offerings to this House." It was Judith the Wise who swayed her colleagues, when she stood up in the assembly and said, "There are four things which guarantee that our people will endure: our prayers, our acts of loving kindness, our books, and our dreams."

We know almost nothing about Rachel. Conversely, in *The Testament of Queen Helena* we find an account of an historical figure who we know a great deal about. Helena of Adiabene, who converted to Judaism around the year 30 CE, is remembered by Josephus and in all three Talmuds as a major patron of the Second Temple. Her book is our oldest surviving mystical text, and spiritual seekers still use the three visions that Queen Helena recorded as a ladder for their own mystical experiences.

In terms of enduring popularity, we need look no further than *The Psalms of the Singers of the House of God*. The first one, included in this volume, "As With Birds," has long been recited at baby naming ceremonies for children, and the next one, "Now in Late Spring," is traditionally recited with the Shema on one's deathbed.

Just as the book of *Chronicles* provides an historical summary and conclusion to the three sections of the Hebrew Bible that had already been canonized, the rabbis and sages at the Glorious Assembly unanimously chose as its final volume *The Chronicles of Miriam the Just*. This book, written by Miriam Julia the daughter of Antigonus, the last Maccabeean king, tells the story of the Second Temple era from its foundation until the reign of King Herod and the Roman take-over of Judea.

Since the destruction of the Third Temple in 537, the books in "Zichronot" have been one of our greatest comforts. Rabbi Irmgard Baum called these ten sacred books, "Our fourth temple in words, a balm in times of Job-like sorrow," and reminds us that, "Just as we come back to Spring again and again, these ancient books are surely a guide to our eternal renewal." May your reading of the excerpts below be a blessing.

THE VISIONS OF RACHEL THE DREAMER

We know almost nothing about the author of this remarkable book, including her name. Scholars suspect that an anonymous work was given its title to conjure the biblical matriarch. The Damascus Talmud informs us of her birth in Hebron under the Maccabeean queen Salome Alexandra, and according to Josephus she was related to the royal family through her mother. If this is accurate we can assume that she had access to the partial education available in that period to women of her class, as well as access to the influence of Greek and Roman ideas, all of which may have shaped her decision to keep a log of her dreams.

Whatever its origins, Rabbi Hannah ibn Daud asserts that, "This book is the revolutionary text that finally brought Jewish women into the conversation." We include five chapters that come from different periods in the life of the author and reflect the source of the gender-balanced God-language which has been a part of our liturgy since that time. It was from the opening chapter of this book, below, that the sages of the Glorious Assembly crafted the famous High Holiday hymn, "Our Father Our King, Our Mother Our Queen" found in every rite, from the Chinese to the Moroccan.

The Dream of the Coin

In the dream I am walking on the Mount of Olives. I stop and sit down on a rock and look down upon the city, upon the temple, in all of its beauty. An undulating cloud of smoke rises up from the innermost court, from the great altar, and as the wind shifts, from time to time, it brings to me softly the words of the priests chanting. As I stand to rise I look down and see on the ground at my feet a tiny gold coin, and I lean down to pick it up. On one side of the coin is the image of a great empty throne. Beneath it, in our ancient Hebrew letters, are the words, "His seat." The reverse, when I turn it over, bears the exact same image of a great empty throne. Beneath it, in the same ancient Hebrew letters, are the words, "Her seat."

When I woke I took up pen and parchment and wrote down that dream, just as you read it.

The Dream of the Tent

In the dream I am a servant, and my mistress, our mother Sarah, calls to me and says, "Hurry, take three measures of fine flour, kneed it, and make cakes from it." I can hear my master Abraham calling to a servant, saying, "Hurry, take this calf, tender and good to eat, and prepare it for a meal." And we do as they say, and when the bread is done and the calf is cooked, the manservant adds curds and spices to the meat in a flat bowl, and I lay out the breads on a large flat plate decorated with flowers. And we run, and we bring them to our master, who is seated in front of his tent in the heat of the day, his tent which stands before the oaks of Mamre. And seated beside him, on soft cushions, are three older women, all of them strangers.

Now my mistress is seated in their tent, but the oldest of the three visitors asks my master, "Where is Sarah your wife?" And he says, "Here in the tent." And the woman, old and so beautiful, turns toward the tent as she speaks to my master, saying, "I shall come back to you in a year, and you and Sarah your wife will have a son." And my master laughs, for he and my mistress are advanced in years, but my mistress says, "Surely this is God, come to bless us in our old age."

And I woke, amazed, knowing that when She returned a year later, that Sarah was holding to her breast our ancestor Isaac. And I wrote down this dream in my scroll, with ink and reed, and rolled it up again when the ink was dry.

The Dream of the Eagle

In the dream I am a great bird, an eagle. I remember what it feels like to look down, not from the top of a hill or a mountain, to look down from the top of the sky. Clouds drift by, and I sail through them. And I remember what it feels like, to take off from my mountain perch, to sail, to soar, to drift on invisible currents, my powerful wings outstretched like those of our Mother.

With unerring intent, following a deep sense of inner wisdom, I set my course toward a distant mountain. I fly and keep flying, and my wings are sore, my body is aching, but there is somewhere that I have to get to, by a certain time. In the distance, the mountain of my quest appears, tall and cutting into the sky. I approach it, exhausted, ready to drop to the ground, but a voice like thunder echoes out across the mountain, saying, "No man may see me and live." And I hear the voice direct Moses to place himself in the

35

cleft of a rock on the top of that mountain, and when he does, She appears, and She passes swiftly by. And while he cannot see Her face, but only see Her from behind, I turn for a moment, not being a man, not even a human, and I see before me a light, a vast light, shining from one end of the heavens to the other. And in the midst of that light—I can see Her face, clearly. But when I awoke I could remember nothing but what I just wrote down, nothing but that which you can read here in this scroll.

The Dream of the Ant

In the dream I am walking up the temple steps toward the Huldah Gates when a voice calls out to me, "Rachel," a blinding voice that fills the heavens and yet narrows itself down to me, like new date honey pouring down through a funnel. "Rachel," She says to me, "An ant could more easily understand you and your life than you can understand Me."

I remain silent, frozen, with fellow pilgrims swarming up and down the stairs around me. I stop, lean a hand on the wall to my right, and wait, for at such moments it doesn't seem right, or even appropriate, to respond. And She goes on, in a voice both rich and resonant, deep and powerful: "At this moment there are more stars in My creation than you or anyone else has words for, in any of the seventy languages of this world, and there are more other worlds with people on them than any of you could ever imagine."

Words come to me and vanish, questions, longings. I want to say something to Her, ask Her something, but a mother with a child on her back bumps into me on the stairs, bows and hurries away, when she sees the faraway look in my eyes. And She goes on, saying, "I am not just the One who created the heavens and the earth. I am Infinite Eternal Creativity. And all that I ask of you is to be creative yourself. And in doing that, you won't understand Me any more than an ant could understand you. But you'll be doing something better. You'll be fulfilling that which was born deep within you, Rachel the daughter of Sarah the daughter of Ahuvah."

Suddenly I am exhausted. I am straining all my senses to keep listening, and my body is trembling, and I am filled with awe, and joy, and fear of Her vastness. Weary, I turn and sit down on the cold marble stairs. And when I woke, the first light of day was whispering itself up over the hills outside my window, and I sighed and stretched and yawned, remembering this strange dream. And I roused myself from my bed, and I took up reed and bottle of ink, and I inscribed this dream on my long tall roll of imported Egyptian paper.

The Dream of the Sheep and the Rams

In the dream I am walking through a field of barley when She comes to me. She comes as a soft wind blowing over the field, bowing the sheaves like worshippers in the temple. And this is what She says to me. "Rachel, I told the last of My prophets, hundreds of years ago, that I was tired of sacrifices, burnt offerings, your new moons and holidays. Amos and Isaiah heard Me. Hosea and Jeremiah grasped what I was telling them too, that what I want from you is goodness and not the sacrifice of sheep, rams, cattle, birds, cakes, or wine. I want from you righteousness and not good incense."

She continues to speak to me, saying, "And now you have synagogues in addition to a temple, you have prayers that you recite to Me, thinking that I require them, that they please Me. But I have no interest in your holidays. I'm bored by your services and by the hollow words that come pouring from your mouths like up-flowing rain. What I want from you is not words but acts of loving kindness, what I want from you are tenderness and comfort, not Torah chanters and large loud choruses. And yet, in spite of everything, I have always loved you and I always will. I created you and every day, in each and every moment, I am speaking to you, reaching out to you, to all of you, without exception. But every day, you get so caught up in your old rituals that you don't hear Me. But there is one small inner place where you can always find Me, in a place much better than words."

And then She is gone, and in the place of Her words—all there is is silence, a vast silence. But in the midst of the silence I can feel Her, and I woke up, and it was the dark of night, and there were stars but no moon outside my window. And I lay awake in my soft bed till morning came, and its sweet light. Then I took out reed and ink and wrote these words down, for all of you, my children.

THE TESTAMENT OF QUEEN HELENA

In the third decade of the Common Era, Helena, the queen of Adiabene, a small vassal state on the Upper Tigris in the Parthian Empire, converted to Judaism along with her sons Izates and Monobaz. Mentioned by Josephus and in all three Talmuds for her piety and generosity, Helena made numerous gifts to the temple and imported food from Egypt and Cyprus during a famine in Palestine. She lived in Jerusalem for many years, and although she died in Adiabene, she was buried in the holy city, in a grave plowed under and lost to us after the destruction of the Third Temple.

Her book begins by quoting from *Tobit*, and includes references and allusions to *Psalms, Deuteronomy, Ecclesiastes, Ezekiel, Isaiah, Micah*, and *Zephaniah*, along with themes that link it to later Jewish mystics and their visions of God's chariot, making it the earliest known of our mystical texts, of which echoes can be heard in the ones that follow, all the way down to the *Zohar*.

1

I, Helena, a daughter of Ahuvah, walked in the ways of truth and performed many acts of charity for my people, and yet, two nights before the beginning of the great festival of Tabernacles, my heart was heavy and I could not sleep, so I called Deborah my maidservant, who lit four lamps in the lampstand beside my bed. Sitting up, hoping to find comfort, I turned to the scroll of Psalms that had been given to me by my teacher Eliezer ben Simeon, but my eyes skimmed over the words without taking them in, and my mind kept returning to the marketplace that afternoon.

I had made my way to the stalls at the foot of the temple, with Deborah and two attendants, to purchase for our household an *etrog* and the right branches to weave into a *lulav*, a cluster of branches I picked myself, for use during the holiday. Residents and pilgrims were jostling from stall to stall, hunting for bargains, hunting for the perfect *etrog*, well-formed and perfectly colored. Some were nestled in straw, others in cloth, leaves, or sat in neatly carved olivewood boxes. I went directly to the stall of my favorite vender, a man whose family has been growing *etrogs* on the same land for more than two hundred years. As always, he greeted me warmly and pulled from beneath the stall an *etrog* he had been saving for me, resting like an egg in a small silver nest. It was warm in my hands, fragrant, a brilliant yellow, its shape perfect, its stem thick and securely attached. As Deborah paid his assistant, the old man wrapped it up for me in cloth and bowed deeply, thanking me for honoring him once again.

All of that was joyous. It was what followed that haunted me in the night. As Deborah and I turned to go, a burly man in the robes of a minor priest caught my eye and nodded, curtly. As I turned I heard him say to his companion, "She may buy the most expensive fruit in the market and give the greatest tithings to the temple, but when the end of the world comes, she will be counted as a daughter of Persia and not Israel."

I could not tell if he'd said those words thinking that I was out of earshot, or if he said them deliberately, to wound me. Even though Eliezer and later the high priest had reminded me that Pharaoh's daughter had converted, that Ruth, another convert, will be the ancestor of the messiah, and that I myself will have a treasured name among the people of Israel, I still felt a sharp stabbing in my heart. To this day there are families who will not share their tables with me or my sons, and elders and scholars in Jerusalem who have condemned our conversions, in the name of the very same God we all serve.

With a sigh I went back to my scroll, but the words of David the King brought me no comfort. Finally, exhausted, I turned to blow out the lamps, and was startled to see a tall figure standing at the foot of my bed. "Master," I whispered, to the tall familiar form of my old beloved teacher Eliezer, so many years dead and yet standing there before me, in the same brown robe with black stripes that he always wore, as if he were alive.

A gentle smile played across his dark and deeply lined face. "Shema Yisrael," he said. Those words cut through my sorrow and dissolved it. "Hear, Israel." For what I saw in his kind face and heard in his words was the answer to my unspoken prayer. What I heard in those two holy words from Torah was his reminder of my place among our people, his assurance that I too am a part of Israel.

I was both afraid and filled with joy at the same time. "Master," I said to him again, nodding my head, bowing, wanting to thank him for coming to me in my hour of need. But he silenced me with a single gesture, raised his right hand, and pointed his forefinger toward my chest. All at once my heart was filled with a brilliant golden light. Stunned, awed, I brought my hands to my chest, where I could feel a deep pulsing warmth. But when I lifted my eyes to my teacher, wanting to ask him what he had done to me—he was gone. I lay awake till dawn rose softly pink in the sky, feeling and watching that inward light slowly fade, till all that was left was the memory of it, engraved upon my innermost being, on the deepest core of my living breathing flesh.

2

That year during Tabernacles the city was filled with joyous pilgrims, and I opened my home to as many visitors as it could contain. The temple was crowded and I chose to remain at home while my guests joined the throngs of celebrants for the midday sacrifices. During the heat of the first day of the Water-Drawing Festival, I received guests in my audience chamber, old friends and new friends, priests, elders and their families.

Verses from the Scrolls of "Zichronot"

That afternoon, having sent my visitors and guests off to the temple, listening to the sound of people in the streets, I knew that there were men raising stacks of wood in the outer temple courtyard. In a few hours the holy city would be filled with young women and men dancing through the night, seeking their destined mates. And I was filled with a sense of deep sorrow. My own beloved husband had been taken from me, and I sat upon my marble throne, a queen alone, my children miles and miles away in our homeland. All is vanity, it seemed to me, nothingness. I have had my time of joy, and this is the season of my despair. Too much did I love my husband to ever marry again. No, I am alone, soon to return to my empty bedchamber. And just as the day ends, as the sun sinks into the distant sea, I thought, so too do I drift down toward the end of my life.

I sat with my face buried in my hands, and then I heard, slowly moving toward me, the sound of footsteps on the marble floor. I looked up, startled, to see a tall thin woman, a long red shawl draped over her head and thrown across one shoulder, slowly coming toward me. I looked at her, confused and annoyed, for the doors to my audience hall were closed. "Who are you?" I asked her, "and how did you get in here?"

The woman smiled, nodded, and said, with laughter in her voice, "I am Huldah of ancient days, who sat by the stairs leading into the old temple, draped in my cloak and prophesying to all the people."

Had I not seen with my own eyes the solid form of my old master, my beloved teacher, the one who led me to this blessed path, I would not have believed her. But I knew the truth of her words. I could feel it, I could see it in her large dark eyes.

"But why are you here? Why have you come to speak with me in my sorrow, at this time of great rejoicing?"

Instead of answering my questions, Huldah said to me two Hebrew words, the next two words of our most sacred prayer, beginning where Eliezer left off. I was stunned, for in saying them she pronounced the holy name of God that schoolboys whisper among themselves, that everyone knows but only the high priest says aloud, once a year, in the Holy of Holies, while the rest of us say in its stead, "Adonai," Our Lord.

"YHWH Elohenu," she said. "YHWH is our God." And in that moment I understood—that she had come to remind me that my longing for my dear departed husband had filled the chambers of a heart that could now be devoted to the Divine Beloved, to God, to the Lord of all creation.

Again, my aching heart was comforted by an unexpected visitor. But instead of vanishing as Eliezer had, the prophetess took a step toward me and raised her hands in front of her, palms uplifted. Then she spread them in an arc in front of me and it was as if she had removed by that gesture the scales that covered my eyes. I could see all around me a radiant golden light that filled my audience chamber. Looking out the open windows to my garden I saw that it too was aglow. And into the midst of that golden light Huldah stepped—and vanished, just as Eliezer had, right before my eyes.

I rose and walked to the windows. Although it was not yet evening, the garden, the city beyond it, and the sky above it as far as I could see, were bathed in that brilliant golden light. I knew it was a supernal light that I was able to see, the primal light that God created on the very first day of creation. Trembling, I sank to my knees in silent prayer, watching the light till it slowly faded from around and before me.

3

Near the end of the Feast of Tabernacles, on the last evening of the Water-Drawing Festival, in the last hours of the day, I sat beneath an arbor on the roof of my palace, looking out on the city, a spool of golden thread lying in a sea of white in my lap. Transfixed by the spiraling smoke rising up from the innermost courtyard of the temple, I knew that the priests were beginning the evening offerings. How curious, I often thought when I stood in the women's balcony of the temple—how before my conversion, as queen of my people, I had access to all of the holy places in our land. And

Verses from the Scrolls of "Zichronot"

yet here where my heart belongs, even though the high priest has called me a pious woman in Israel, I am excluded from the innermost courtyard and the temple itself.

The mingled odors of sacrifice and sweet incense wafted up and over the roof, and for a moment in the stillness I could faintly hear the chanting of the priestly choir. Content again, I took up the spool of golden thread and turned back to my work. Spread out in my lap was a robe of the purest white silk, a robe whose collar I was embroidering, the robe a gift for the high priest to wear the following day for Hoshanah Rabbah.

Needle in hand, I went back to my task, weaving around the collar with delicate stitches a tendril of grape vines. Branch by branch, leaf by leaf, I had been working on this project for weeks. The gold thread, imported from Rome, was difficult to work with, and the fine fine cloth, come all the way from China, was so delicate that a needle piercing it in the wrong place could easily damage it. Needing to concentrate, I had requested that no one disturb me except in an emergency, as I wanted to finish before the last light faded, the new day began, and before I went in to dine with my guests.

I stitched in another leaf, another bit of vine, then another leaf. But suddenly, as we sometimes do, I felt that someone was standing behind me, and I turned, afraid that something untoward had occurred. Standing there—no, that is not the right word, for he was not standing at all but floating in air a hand's breadth above the floor—was a messenger of God, a luminous angel cloaked in white, his large golden wings spread out behind him. I call this angel he, and yet there was nothing male in his form—nor anything female either. He or she was not unlike the many eunuchs of my father's court, both female and male, and yet neither.

Remembering the hospitality of Abraham and Sarah, I was about to call to my servants to bring him food, but the angel silenced me with a swift gesture and then bid me to rise with a voice that I heard in the middle of my mind. I put down my sewing, rose, and moved toward the angel. Then it spread its wings and stepped toward me, wrapped me in its arms and carried me aloft, over the city, up and over the great shining outer walls of the temple courtyard, circling till we came to the court of the priests. I could see them below me, offering the evening sacrifices, as the angel swooped low and carried me above the curved stairs to the entrance of the temple, through the Porch into the Holy Place, through the great blue and purple curtain, right into the Holy of Holies. Then we shot up from there, that dark empty space, up through the roof till we were high above the temple, its courts packed full with pilgrims.

Only later did I wonder why I wasn't afraid. People do not swoop and soar like birds, and yet there I was, high above the spiraling smoke of the offerings, so high above that I could not hear the sound of the priests chanting, nor the voices of the worshippers responding. And there it was beneath me, the vast complex designed by King Herod, with work still being done upon it, which is already one of the largest and grandest temples in the world.

Then there was a great silent wind and I could hear everywhere around me, echoing off the edges of the cosmos, the last two words of our most sacred prayer. I cannot bring myself to say them as I heard them, cannot bring myself to say God's holy name. I can only say the last words of this prayer: "Adonai Echad—The Lord is One."

I expected to see, as had the prophets of old, a vision of God upon His heavenly throne. But instead, all at once, the light in my heart began to shine and the light in the world blazed up again, and I knew that the two lights were the same, a radiant golden light that fills all of creation and ripples on forever. And I knew that I had always heard those words incorrectly. I had heard them as, "The God that we worship is the only God there is." But there, high above the temple, above the city, high above the world, looking down upon on it, bathed in golden light and filled with it, I knew what those words really mean: "This God that we call The Lord is the living heart of a greater Unity that we can name Echad, One." I knew that all is One, from and in and One with this Being whose eternal infinite Oneness is greater than any human being can ever understand or imagine.

As the truth of those words penetrated to the very center of my own heart, I found myself back on the roof of my palace, sitting in my chair, with my sewing on the little golden table beside me. I turned, looking around me for the angel, but it was gone. Nor have I seen my teacher Eliezer, or the prophetess Huldah, or that nameless angel again, in all of these ten years since that feast of Tabernacles.

And this is my testament as I lay dying, given to my youngest son Hananiah to write on parchment. These are the words of a pious lady, who was blessed to see what few have seen before—the light of the One who created the world, Who has shown faithfulness to Israel, and raised me up and renewed me in love on a day of festival.

May these words be a blessing to all who read them.

THE PSALMS OF THE SINGERS OF THE HOUSE OF GOD

This little book of psalms remains the most popular scroll in "Zichronot," used daily in private and public worship. The first psalm in the collection, "As with Birds," has long been recited at baby naming ceremonies, and the next one, "Now in Late Spring," is traditionally recited with the Shema on one's deathbed. Many of these psalms and prayers, which alternate in addressing God as male and female, have also entered our communal liturgy, including the eight prayers to "Our Mother Wisdom," which are sung at the beginning and end of the Sabbath.

These 150 psalms are clearly meant to parallel the 150 psalms found in the book of that name in the third section of the Bible, but even in ancient times there was debate about their origins and usage. Rabbi Ruth of Ashdod in the Alexandrian Talmud states that these psalms were recited by the Levites in the Second Temple, however Jacob the Priest is quoted in the Damascus Talmud as saying that this second collection of psalms were written by women who sang them in the outer temple courtyard, the "singers at the entrance to the tabernacle" who are mentioned in the books of *Samuel* and *Ezra*.

Rabbi Italo Nassim Schwartz claims that the last ten psalms, which praise the Persian emperor Cyrus the Great for allowing the exiled Jews to return from Babylon and rebuild the Second Temple, were actually written in the very early Third Temple era to celebrate Emperor Julian. Rabbi Sarah Tagawa has shown linguistically that the entire book is indeed a product of the Second Temple era, chosen from thousands of other songs and prayers that may have been recited in that temple to reflect the joy of the return and rebuilding of the Third. As was pointed out by 5th century Rabbi Sophia of Thebes, Psalm 127—"Thank You My Dear," paraphrases one of Sappho's poems, which she addressed to a lover and the psalmist addresses to the God Herself.

From this collection we have included eight psalms, which reflect the range of themes in this cherished book, with gratitude to Rabbi Miriam Rodrigawitz of Temple Shalom in Antarctica for allowing us to use her luminous contemporary translations.

Psalm 1—As With Birds

On the first day You created light
O bless me Lord with Your light
and on the second day You divided the waters
O bless me Lady with Your waters
For I stagger in darkness, thirsty for Your love
and You come to me as on the third day
creating plants and trees to feed me
for I am hungry, and I yearn for You.
Then sun and moon and stars You set above my head
O Lord of all
O Lady our Mother
who brings life to the sea and to the sky
and as with birds, wings spread and soaring
I raise my arms in song and praise to You
O Most High
and as with birds I lift my heart up toward You
in whose heart all worlds endure forever.
Amen. Amen. Selah.

Verses from the Scrolls of "Zichronot"

Psalm 2—Now in Late Spring

New green has darkened
boughs once bare are heavy laden
and my heart, once empty
is now full of You, O God of all that is
and I call out Your name
Mother of Life
and like a tree, a tree of life
You open Your sheltering arms to me
and there I find comfort
and there I find rest.
Amen.

Psalm 34—Now That Night Has Fallen

There is no moon and the stars, forlorn
shine, but they shine in desperation
and my heart is like those stars
and I call out to You in the darkness
but You do not answer
and the fire at my feet flickers
and I say to myself—surely You have abandoned me
and the tears that fall from my eyes
are each another prayer
unanswered.
Why did You make us and place us here?
And why do You abandon us
again and again?
Are we orphans, cast away?
Or are we Your beloved children?
The night is long and I am afraid.
Come to me now, my Secret Lover
come to me now and comfort me.

Psalm 99—Your Laughter

I asked You for a sign
as I stood before Your altar
and the wind turned
and the smoke blew in my face
stinging my eyes
making me gasp for breath
and I hated You for abandoning me
but then You came to me with Your Laughter
saying
"This is your sign my beloved child.
No Moses you are, no Miriam.
I come to you in this small small way."
And I laughed then with You
and I am laughing still
with wet and burning eyes.

Psalm 127—Thank You My Dear

I wake in the morning and turn to You
Your arms still around me as I stretch
and I thank You my dear
for You came to me when I needed You
and You have made love blaze up in my breast
and I am blessed by You
now and in all the hours of my life
for You are One
and I am one in Your embrace.

Psalm 129—Like a Lover

I wake in the darkness and hear him
breathing softly beside me.
Our pillow shifts slowly as his head rolls gently.
I cannot see him
although the image of his face
in my mind's loving eye makes me smile.
So like You when You come to me

VERSES FROM THE SCROLLS OF "ZICHRONOT"

       touch me
 in the light of late afternoon
 sun low in the sky behind trees
     their leaves lit golden
         as if from within.
   Yet even in that golden light
         I cannot see You
 just as now I cannot see him in the darkness
     but I feel him, hear him
     breathing softly beside me.
          In out. Out in.
           Like You God
         the Breath Giver.

Psalm 135—The Opposite of a Thief

    You are the opposite of a thief
    slipping into the house of mind
           when I'm out
           to leave me
       exactly what I wanted.

Psalm 150—Transcending Angels

       Now transcending angels
        I sit in Your presence.
              There
          all texts vanish,
          all given books,
          all dictated words.
              Only
       the singing of my heart
              remains,
       surrounded by stillness
           like golden ink
         on a jet-black page.

4
The Five Books of Motion

In 2011 Shira Mendosa, the director of the Mechol'el Dance Theatre of the West, invited me to write a series of stories for the company to work with, to be called "The Five Books of Motion." Her idea was that each piece would be done to different music, in a different style, danced by different members of the company.

After our first conversation I sketched out a five-part performance that would play with Jewish texts and Jewish history, beginning with a story set in India in the trade colony established by King Solomon. It was about a merchant in the years after the First Temple was destroyed who goes off to study with a new teacher, the Buddha. But no matter how many versions I wrote, I couldn't bring the story to life. Then I tried to retell one of my favorite stories in the Bible, about Job, from his wives' perspectives, but I couldn't make that work either. Finally Shira suggested that I go back to the Torah and requested something edgy that would reflect the company. I went home and wrote what became the opening piece, about Moses and Joshua, which was danced to a bold fusion of electronic music and Middle Eastern songs.

My second story idea began with regret. Shortly after the 2010 publication of *Queering the Text,* I realized that I should have written a fourth section, set in Greco-Roman Alexandria in the Second Temple era, with stories about Jewish women who love women who read Sappho. Instead of a series of such stories, I wrote only one, which Shira set to several traditional Greek Jewish folk dances.

The story for the third dance-piece came to me easily. It's set in Third Temple Jerusalem, concerns my grandmother Rosanna's great hero, Judith the Wise, and was danced to a mixture of traditional Syrian and Egyptian Sukkot melodies, with some Bach woven in, from his cello suites.

Given the great interest in Buddhism among American Jews, I sketched out a story about two yeshiva boys in 17th century Kaifeng, China who fall in love with Buddhist texts and with each other, but I couldn't make it work. What did work was traveling further back in time to Cordoba, Spain during the Golden Age, when it was the world's largest city and had a flourishing Jewish community. The company was excited about dancing to a series of traditional Sephardic songs with some tango floating through.

I knew that I wanted the last piece to take place in San Francisco, and presented Shira and the company with four stories: about Levi-Strauss and the Gold Rush, the Great Quake of 1958, Allen Ginsberg and the Beats, and one set in our own time, about Shabbat and the kinds of people we all know. When I read them to the company, everyone liked the last one, especially after they heard the music Shira put together for it, a mix of rock, hip-hop, and klezmer.

The show premiered in San Francisco in March of 2013 and went on tour for four months. Instead of formal sets, each piece was danced in front of projected text, images, and short videos that suggested the varied locations. If you haven't seen the show, you can go to WeTube and watch the San Francisco premiere, and also read a wonderful online review in the *New York Times* about the opening performance at the Brooklyn Academy of Music on July 34, 2013.

SINAI—IN A PILLAR OF CLOUD

Moses pushed aside the opening to his tent, as the lapis sky of night gave way to sapphire. His worn robe flapping on burly legs, Moses hurried toward the Tent of Meeting. The camp was still quiet. Here and there, women and girls were squatting next to small fires, to prepare their meager meals. At the far end of the camp a baby was crying. In the hills a wild dog began to bay, and a second one answered.

Caleb was sitting in front of his small tent, watching the sun rise up over the distant hills, as Moses strode by, without seeing him. "So it's true," Caleb said out loud, as the older man passed, his sandals slapping on sand. Two days before, when Caleb approached the altar, the men who were gathered there stopped talking. He knew they'd been talking about him, and about Moses and Joshua. Joshua, who no longer looked at him the way he used to, who pulled back the last time Caleb reached out to touch him. He'd wanted to believe Joshua when he said it was because Moses had asked him to move into the Tent to be its guard, that it was a time of purification. No, he *had* believed him, in his mind, but not in his body. And now, at sunrise, watching Moses race toward the Tent, smiling, every part of him knew the truth. Rage washed through Caleb's body. He had lost Joshua, his friend, lover, his brother of the heart. There was a large stone lying at his feet. He bent, grabbed it, and hurled it into the air, down the path that Moses had taken. "I'll get him back," he shouted in his mind. "And when I do, old man, we'll leave you in the dust! We'll dig you a shallow grave and bury you where no one will ever find you!" But as the stone flew from his hands, so too did his rage. He collapsed into himself, fell to his knees in the barren earth, and began to sob, doubled over, his face buried in his hands.

Through the opening to the Tent of Meeting a column of incense rose up, snaking its way into the clear morning sky. Like a branching tree the incense spread, like a billowing vertical river. Moses saw it rising as he slipped off his sandals, bowed, and entered the tent. And in the Tent of Meeting, the young man Joshua stood before the golden incense altar, his hands stretched toward the burning coals and the silver rising cloud of fragrant offering. Incense filled the holy place as Moses stepped closer to the spirit-filled youth, just as his father-in-law Jethro had stepped toward him, smiling, all those years ago. And the two of them embraced there, Moses and Joshua, forming a new link in the chain of transmission, older to younger, generation to generation. And the cloud surrounded them and enfolded them, until the two became one, one in the presence of the One who created us all.

ALEXANDRIA—THE HIDDEN TEXT

Hearing footsteps in the hallway, Mariamne quickly rolled up the scroll she was reading and slid it behind a cushion on the divan—but not quickly enough. Fortunately it was her sister Arsinoë, laughing as she came in, her sandals slapping on the pink and black marble checked floor.

"What are you reading?"

"Don't tell Father. Sappho."

"Why would he mind? When he's not reading Torah he's reading Plato."

"Because of Hathor."

"The goddess?"

"Don't be silly. Hathor down the street. Mother told me that I have to stop spending time with her. That people are talking."

"People always talk, but no one talks as much as Mother."

Arsinoë, two years younger than her sister, sat beside her on the divan, and the two of them began to laugh.

"Mother is so old fashioned," younger sister said to older.

"She's from Jerusalem, not from here. What do you expect? She grew up on Hebrew and Torah and hasn't been able to get beyond them."

"He may be strict at times, but at least Father is modern. I'd die if we had to live in Jerusalem. Moses was lucky that he didn't get to cross over to the promised land."

"I agree. Whenever we go there to visit, I can't wait to get back. Alexandria is the center of the world, and Jerusalem . . ."

"Is filled with boring people and boring prayers, and the smoke of burned-up animals is always blowing in your eyes."

"Mother would go berserk if she heard you."

"Mother tells strangers in the market that her brother is the high priest. Like anyone cares."

"Here, not even the Jews care."

"So read me what you were reading."

Mariamne slipped her hand behind the cushion and pulled out the small parchment scroll.

"This one's from a series of ten poems Sappho wrote about one of her rivals."

> Unshackled, she comes toward me in the marketplace.
> "Darling," she says, "it's been so long that you
> once obsidian shiny bright
> have bested yourself and
> become the night sky streaked with shooting stars.
> I turn to her, smiling, shoulder weighted down by . . .

"I don't understand it."

"Of course you do. Last week I read you another poem about her rival. Don't you remember her name?"

Arsinoë looked down at the floor.

"Her name was the same as the woman we read about with Father, from one of the Greek stories. The one who was chained to a rock. Andromeda."

"So that's what 'Unshackled' means. But what about the obsidian?"

"Think about it, Arsi. What color is obsidian?"

"Black."

"Once obsidian shiny bright, you have bested yourself and become . . ."

"I get it! She's saying, 'Sappho, you're hair is turning gray.'"

"Exactly!"

"That's way better than the Psalms. Father has me memorizing them again. I can understand his insistence that there's only one god, but if it were up to me, I would have chosen Isis."

"Or Hathor!"

"You and your Hathor."

"You told me you thought she was pretty."

"I do. But she's not very smart."

"What do I need a smart girlfriend for, when I have a brilliant sister?"

"Because we're going to be married off to rich men who will swell us up with babies, year after year, for their greater glory."

"I refuse to allow myself to be married off like a slave girl."

"You're descended from a long line of priests, you're the niece of the high priest, and your Uncle Philo is a famous philosopher. So you'll be married off like Queen Esther. And no one will ask you what you want. But if you're lucky, Father will sneak you copies of Plato and Aristotle, but even he won't dare to bring you Sappho. And that's the only freedom you'll get. And you know that as well as I do, my dear big sister."

"Arsinoë, I can't believe you. We're living in modern times. This isn't our mother's generation. And nobody is going to marry us off."

"Come on, Mariamne. They've been trying for years. And we can't keep putting them off. As Father says, we're not getting any younger. And they've got it all planned out. I heard Mother talking about it with Aunt Leah. You are going to fat cousin Alexander Judah, and I am going to Julius the dimwitted son of the priest in that silly fake temple in Leontopolis."

"No, I am going to run off to one of those Essene communities in the desert, where the women all live freely."

"And celibate!"

"How do you know that?"

"I read it in Uncle Philo's new book."

"Well Hathor and I haven't gone all the way yet, but . . ."

"You only like Hathor because she's not Jewish."

"I liked Shulamit!"

"That's because Rachel told you how good she kisses."

"If Mother and Father could hear us now."

"They would die."

"It's a good thing that Salome and Hyrcanus and Jonathan all have kids. They can't pin all of that grandchildren stuff on us."

"What's the chance of one family having two daughters who like girls?"

"You know what our wonderful uncle says—'It's a Greek affliction. Our girls don't have it.'"

"That's because he always has his nose buried in some book. Otherwise he'd know that it was his own lovely daughter Rachel who corrupted both of us."

"Thank God!"

"Which one? Adonai? Elohim? El Shaddai?"

"Yours and my favorite—El Isis."

"But do you think that there will ever be a Jewish Sappho?"

"There must have been, and there will be again—if *you* keep writing!"

"Well, we've put off getting married for this long. Maybe we can keep going."

"Boys have it so easy. Jonathan had sex with Simeon every afternoon for years, and no one said a thing."

"That's because boys can whip it out in a corner and get off so fast that no one notices."

"But in the end the parents still married him off to that annoying Bernice."

"Well I supposed marriage is better than being a virgin priestess."

"I think virgin just means not being with men. Those priestesses are probably making it with each other all the time. You've seen them, on holidays when they parade through the city. No one could look that happy and be a middle-aged virgin."

"It's the drugs they do."

"It's the hot new girls they recruit."

"Do you really think so?"

"Read me another one of those poems."

"Here's one of my favorites. It's way better than that *Song of Songs* Father likes to read to us on Shabbat."

> The way your shawl falls over your shoulder
> Andromeda
> like water over the rocks of a descending stream
> here clinging to your body

there concealing it
here covering your breasts
there baring your lovely throat
so beautiful that
for a moment
I forget everything and think
Amphitrite or one of her Nereids
has come to sit beside me
for a while
her fragrance
scenting the air

then I remember Atthis
and how you took her from me
and the hand
that began to open to yours
like a crocus
moves slowly toward your
swan-like throat

"What if Huldah the Prophetess wrote things like that, but the priests and prophets threw them out?"

"Maybe someday someone will find them buried in an old trash heap."

"That's how life is. The beautiful and the sordid pressed together."

"Don't remind me of Cleo."

"In the beginning you liked her sordidness."

"I guess I have limits. I am, after all, a nice Jewish girl."

"There. You said it. Some things cannot be gotten away from. And the parents would be so happy to hear you say that."

"Speaking of which . . ." they both turn toward the sound of footsteps in the hall. Mariamne slips the scroll back behind her sister.

"Mother! We were just talking about how glad we are that we're Jewish."

"Of course you're glad, girls. Your uncle is the high priest. Your grandfather was the high priest. And even though we don't live in Jerusalem, we belong to the Diploston Synagogue, the largest one in the entire world. What's not to feel glad about?"

Arsinoë turns to her sister and rolls up her eyes.

"Not being a high priestess?"

Their mother froze in the doorway, horrified. "Our people don't have priestesses."

Mariamne cut her off. "What's for dinner, Mother?"

"I invited your cousin Julius. He's in town for the week."

"Mother, have you ever read Sappho?" Arsinoë asked her.

"Of course not! Sappho is forbidden."

"And have you ever eaten pork?"

"Never."

"Shrimp, or crab?"

"Not even the night your father and I were invited to the palace by the queen."

"They say she's lovely."

"Like a goddess."

"Now you sound like Sappho, Mother," Mariamne replied.

"My father would die if he heard you talking."

"Your father *is* dead."

"You know what I mean."

"And you know what we mean," Arsinoë added. "We're Jews of the future. We don't sacrifice animals to our God. We pray, in a brand new synagogue that's so big that someone has to stand in the middle of the prayer hall to signal the people in back with cute little flags when it's time to say Amen."

Their mother looked back and forth, from daughter to daughter, not sure if what her youngest one just said to her was said in jest. But Arsinoë looked up at her with big dark earnest eyes. "All right, dear. Read me some Sappho. Just don't tell your father."

Mariamne once again pulls the scroll out from behind the cushion.

> Tonight
> the moon is lying on the horizon
> on her side
> and I remember the night you lay beside me

    on your side
    running your fingertips over my face
    reciting Homer

"Your Father loves Homer. He says it's just like reading the Torah."

"That's what it's all about, Mother. Loving with all our heart."

"Is that from Sappho?"

"No, it's from the verses we recite right after the Shema."

"Then I suppose it's all right. Read me some more of this Sappho. I like it."

JERUSALEM—HOW CAN THIS BE?

To my esteemed colleague, Rabbi Joshua the son of Ezra,

In your kind letter which arrived today, you ask me to tell you how I, Judith the daughter of Gamaliel, came to my position, wondering as I am sure you and your fellow rabbis in the North must be wondering, how it is that I have for the last many years been both rabbi and the head of a yeshiva, something that is not the custom for women in your part of the world.

Let me answer your question in the most simple fashion, as I have answered others who have asked it of me. My father, of blessed memory, Rabbi Gamaliel the son of Hillel, raised me as a princess in Israel, and also educated me as a good Roman citizen. As the only daughter, from an early age I was given the same education as my three brothers. We were immersed in learning, in Hebrew, Aramaic, Greek, and Latin. Our earliest companions were not other children but the scholars of our community and the sages of our past, and you know the honored position to which my brother Judah has ascended, as Patriarch of our people.

We are far to the south of you, in the land of our ancestors, in the city that has been our capital since the time of King David. We look to you, our long ago scattered kin, carried away by the Babylonians when they conquered Judah and destroyed the glorious temple built by King Solomon. We honor your history as our cousins, we honor your ways, and we know that while our customs may be different from yours, we are all rooted in the same sacred texts. From the time that I could read my father taught me Torah and the wisdom of our sages, taught me how to read the texts of the mystics in the time of the Second Temple, and then he and I would meditate together, as the sages tell us the wise ones of old did for an hour before they prayed.

But do not think that my father had no opposition.

My mother often wailed, "Who will marry her?" How will she ever survive?"

To which my father would answer, "Would you have me throw away an uncut gem? God would never forgive us."

So it was that books and words became my home. The recipes I learned were scholarly, legal, from Torah and our later holy texts, including the *Mishnah* compiled by our ancestor Judah the Prince. My mother would sigh to my father, "Gamaliel, you will turn her into some kind of hybrid creature, neither female nor male, and because of that, good for the work of neither." To which my father would gently take her hand and tenderly reply, "Beloved, our daughter is a treasure, as wise as all of her brothers, and God will surely take care of her."

My mother was herself a wise woman, may her memory be for a blessing. It was to her that the women of our community came for advice, and yet there were times when she would stand in the open doorway to my father's study, listening to our lessons, her brow furrowed. Once, over dinner, I remember her moaning to my father, "Thousands and thousands of priests and prophets, but who can we name among women? Only Miriam and Deborah." To which my father answered: "And Sarah, Rebecca, Rachel and Leah. The five daughters of Zelophehad. And Deborah, Hannah, Huldah, Noadiah, Esther, Salome Alexander, Beruriah, Yalta, Ima Shalom, and your own great ancestor, Queen Helena. Wise women all of them, strong and powerful." To which my mother could do nothing but lift her hands above her head and raise her face to the heavens, with a look in her deep green eyes that said, "I leave this in Your hands."

After many years of studying the books of Moses my father began to teach me from the books of the Prophets, and then from the sacred Writings of our Holy Scriptures. For a year I read the book of *Joshua*, of its wars and its conquest. Then the following year, I turned to the book of the *Judges*. I rejoiced upon reading the "Song of Deborah," so like on a page the great "Song of the Sea," with its broken lines in *Exodus* like surging waves and in *Judges* like the ranks of advancing soldiers. Feeling like a Deborah myself, although I was not yet of the age to be a woman, I went on to read of Gideon and his successors, and I remember the day when I came upon the story of Jephthah, and his wars, and how he sacrificed his unnamed daughter to God, to keep the vow that he had made to God.

Book in one hand, oil lamp in the other, for it was the middle of the night, I went storming down the hallway to my father's study, where I could see a dim light under the door. I knocked, I went in, waving the text in my hand. "How," I demanded of my father, "how could Jephthah have done what he did? Didn't he read the story of the binding of Isaac, or the prohibitions in the Torah on sacrificing sons and daughters?" My father looked up at me from his study table, its surface covered with scrolls. He was silent for a long time, which was very unlike him. "Or," I shouted, "are daughters different to our people than sons, even daughters who come dancing like Miriam with her timbrel?"

Father cited verses from early rabbis who were as distressed by that story as I was, and believed it was a violation of the Torah. But I was too upset and wasn't listening. Later we would go over the verses together, read passages from the sages and from other texts that state that she wasn't actually sacrificed, and I came to understand more than I had before of our teachings. In my anger you might say that I revealed my youth. But by the light of flickering lamps that night, in my anger, I found the heart of my vocation, coming to it wholly and fully, as Ruth the ancestor of David came fully to our people.

One of my study partners was my cousin, Asher the son of Abraham from Tiberias, may his memory be for a blessing. After my father ordained him, the two of us were betrothed. Knowing of my learning, my father placed into our *Ketubah* the provision that I must not be engaged in any housework, lest it distract from my studies, and my betrothed willingly agreed. We continued to study together, and when my father knew that I was ready, with the approval of the other rabbis and of the priests who were helping to build our Third Temple, I myself was ordained a rabbi, the first woman to be so honored in Israel. In the years that followed, Asher and I married, and like our first parent Ahuvah, I brought into the world four children, who were taught together by my husband and me, just as I and my brothers were. At my father's death, the community voted for me to take over as the head of our yeshiva, in the shadow of our grand new shining temple, and there we taught for some years, my husband and I, till his early death.

You ask me in your kind letter, Rabbi, where in Torah I find justification for my position. I have searched my memory and scoured that holy text from the creation of the universe to the death of Moses, and nowhere can I find any mention of rabbis or of yeshivas at all. And yet we are proud of our rabbis, as I know you are of yours. My family is proud to be descended from not just from Queen Helena on my mother's side, but also from the great first Rabbi Hillel on my father's side, as well as from a great scholar of our people who should herself have been ordained a rabbi, the wise Beruriah. And this, dear colleague, is my lineage, tracing all the way back to our ancient leader, David the king.

Again, good Rabbi, I thank you for your kind and generous letter, written on behalf of the rabbis of your nation. I send them and you and your families and all of our communities in the north thoughtful regards from the south, as well as sending you all deep wishes for the very best, as we slowly move toward the new year.

Judith the daughter of Gamaliel and Shoshana
of the family of Ahuvah
The second of Elul
in the thirty-sixth year of our Third Holy Temple

CORDOBA—THE ARTIST IN HIS STUDIO

Rabbi Judah crossed the large well-lit room, avoiding any contact with my cluttered tables as he headed toward me. "Why do artists work in such chaos, and why do they dress so badly?" he asked. "You would think that anyone who makes beautiful things would work in beauty and put on beautiful things."

I wondered if he was testing me, by insulting me in my own studio. I imagined that he had never before been in an artist's workshop, but spent his days in the house of study, surrounded all day by piles of books and rows of students.

"Artists are far sighted," I replied. "We can't see things in front of us, or in mirrors." He said that was ridiculous, as he came closer. I said it was because an artist is always at work, and doesn't want to soil good clothing. "Why not put on a smock or an apron?" he asked. I looked at his long deep red robe, its hem embroidered with golden cresting waves. Around his shoulders was a deep orange cloak, it too embroidered, with intricate designs that I wanted to copy. I bowed to him as he approached, bowed to the head of our community. He bowed back and gave me a probing look. Behind his eyes I could see the thought: "Is this the man who can make beautiful our new synagogue?" He looked me up and down again, and for a moment I feared that my choice, to show my worth and dedication to this amazing and long dreamed of project by wearing my working clothes—had been a miscalculation. I should have worn a better robe, and should have met him in his own home, brought sketches with me, and not invited him here to my studio. The job of a lifetime—evaporating before my eyes. Mind racing, wondering what I could do to redeem myself, these words burst from my lips: "It's because we like to make beauty, not be it." A subtle smile appeared, bent at first to the right, which then spread across his face. He laughed, dark eyes twinkling, reached out a hand and placed it on my shoulder. "Come," he said. "Show me your sketches. I was with the vizier this morning, and he has granted formal approval."

Torah Told Different

I sighed, and bowed again, relieved. If the clothing of an artist cannot be trusted, how much less so his words? I looked around my studio, seeing it for a moment through the rabbi's eyes, the piles, the clutter, the half-finished projects, drawings, carvings, sculptures, all commissioned projects, and the far table in the rear, covered with the special projects of my own, my own little carvings and designs. Yes, I saw the chaos he saw, and at the same time I knew that my sketches would assure him, that just as God had brought forth the world from chaos, that I could bring forth for us from chaos a house of prayer, our very first in the capital.

A small round table of wood in a far corner. Two carved chairs—that had been in our family for generations, their plain backs and seats covered with dark green embroidered cushions made for them by my grandmother, now worn and yet still beautiful. He paused before he took a seat, and nodded—at the table, the hammered copper cups, the silver jug of wine, the small silver plate of flatbreads, an identical plate of sliced fennel root, and a third plate piled with deep purple grapes, the plate pale bone in color and ringed with deep green grape leaves under a heavy glaze. I bowed again and waved a hand, offering him the corner, the carefully set table, the chairs, simple and familiar. Smiling, he took a seat, absorbed in the small tableau that I had created for him.

He was silent for quite some time. Was he thinking what I was thinking? That we may pray facing toward Jerusalem, but that this has been our home for so long that our hearts are here. And did he know, as I offered him wine from a silver jug of simple design, in a simple cup as well—that these cups and jug are of my own design? And was he thinking, as I was, "This for the worship of God, this for our people."

I sat across from him when he was settled, his cloak adjusted, his robe spread out across his lap. And I reached behind me for a sheaf of pages, old ones and the drawings I'd been working on since first his assistant had come to me with the possibility that we might soon be granted our request to build a new and modern synagogue. Respectfully, I handed to the rabbi my grandmother's old sketches on parchment. He slowly flipped through them, page by large page, tears welling up in his eyes.

We all grow up on the stories of our great temples, our three glorious temples, so long before destroyed. We all grow up on stories about the last one—the broad triumphal stairs leading up to it, the great outer court, its marble columns so tall and beautiful in the Jerusalem sun. We all know about the curved stairs up to the inner courtyard through golden doors, and the high altar, and the great House of God itself, soaring up above the city, all marble white and fluted gold. But unlike his family, of scholars and rabbis, who all followed the ban on making images given to us in the commandments, that ban enforced by our Muslim rulers—my family are architects and artisans, artists and designers; so in secret, of course, my artist grandmother, not a teacher or a storyteller, did what any artist would do—she recorded for herself a series of drawings of that vanished temple, just as she had been told about it, just as he imagined it.

A single tear slid down Rabbi Judah's right cheek, paused for a moment on the edge of his ruddy beard, then slid down between thick curly hairs, where he brushed it down with the back of his right hand. And I could hear his unasked question.

"My honorable grandmother did them, many years ago. Rabbis and yeshiva students conjure the past in words. But an artist conjures by sight, by colors and lines. These drawings are visual midrash, they are picture-stories that my grandmother passed on to my father, who passed them on to me." Any fear I had that he, our rabbi, would order me to destroy them, vanished, as he pushed them neatly back into a pile in front of him with his dry left hand, and sighed.

"Rabbi, I wanted you to see them, although I will not show them to anyone else again. Because I want to incorporate elements of the design, the carvings, the moldings, the capitals of the columns, the space and feel of the inner court, into my designs for our new synagogue." And, having said that, I handed him a second set of drawings. Mine.

SAN FRANCISCO—SADIE'S SAME OLD SHABBAT

Sadie was sprawled out on the floor of her bedroom playing a video game when her mother Ruthie called from down the hall, "Sadie, it's almost Shabbat. Will you polish the silver?"

Sadie pushed herself up from the floor with a frown and a groan, and said to herself, out loud, "It's always the same old Shabbat," as she shuffled down the hallway to the kitchen. "And I'm always the one to do the polishing."

Sadie's mother was stirring a big pot on the stove, humming to herself. "Sadie, do you know where the polish is?" her mother asked. Sadie sighed, "Yes I do, Mommy," as she knelt and took out the silver polish from underneath the sink, and then an old rag. Her grandmother's silver Shabbat candlesticks were on the table, right where her mother put them every week after she set it. Kneeling on her chair, Sadie went to work.

Rag in hand she rubbed and buffed and made the first candlestick shiny again. Just as she set it down, the phone rang. "I'll get it," Sadie said, jumping off her chair. "Who was it?" her mother asked a minute later. "Who else? Aunt Deb calling from their car to say that she and Auntie Amrita and the twins are running late. Again."

Sadie was putting the short white Shabbat candles in the candlesticks when the doorbell rang. "I have to check the chicken. Will you get it, Sadie?" her mother asked, leaning over to open the oven door. "Yeah, I'll get it," Sadie mumbled and took off down the hallway, muttering to herself. "It's either Grandpa Sam and Ikuyo, or Uncle Bernie. Nothing ever changes around here. It's always the same old Shabbat."

"Who is it?" Sadie called through the closed door. "It's us," came a very familiar voice. Unlocking the door, Sadie let in her grandfather and his girlfriend Ikuyo, who he met three years before at the JCC in a senior swimming class. Grandpa Sam was leaning on his walker. Ikuyo was carrying a big pink box tied with white string, filled with pastries from her favorite Mexican bakery. "Every week she brings the same old thing," Sadie thought to herself, as her grandfather leaned down to kiss her on the cheek and hug her.

Just as Sadie was about to lock the door she heard the familiar shuffling down the hall that meant Uncle Bernie was there too, a big shopping bag in each hand. "Oh my God, you wouldn't believe the trouble I had finding a parking space. I had to circle the block four times and then I found one, right around the corner, and I was about to..."

Sadie sighed. It was always the same thing with her Uncle Bernie, who wasn't really her uncle but her mother's cousin and best friend going all the way back to their childhood in Brooklyn. "You couldn't even say hello to us?" her grandfather said. "Sorry, Grandpa Sam. Sorry Ikuyo. Shabbat shalom. Shabbat shalom. So anyway, I was just about to pull in when..."

Sadie slid around behind him to lock the door, tuning him out again as he and her grandfather and Ikuyo went down the hall.

"So where are Debra and Amrita and the twins?" Ikuyo asked, as she did every Shabbat. Sadie's mother was carrying bowls of soup to the table as they all came in to the kitchen. "My sister called to say that they're running late." Everyone seemed surprised but Sadie, who sighed to herself, "Every Friday night it's the same old story. What's wrong with all of you grown-ups? Haven't you noticed?"

"Here, let me help you with the soup," Ikuyo offered Ruthie, as Grandpa Sam settled down at the table and Uncle Bernie began pulling food out of his two shopping bags. Sadie winced as for the millionth time tossed spinach salad with tangerine slices in it and a casserole dish of string beans and sliced almonds made their appearance.

"Not on the tablecloth, Bernie. Use a trivet," Sadie's mother cried out. "Ruthie, it's cool already! I've done this every week since Sadie was a baby, and have I ever once burned your mother's tablecloth?" Bernie answered back. Sadie groaned. "At least *he* knows it. It's the same old Shabbat, week after week after week."

Everyone settled in around the table. "How long should we wait for them?" her grandfather asked, as he always did. "A few minutes more," Ruthie answered, as she brought the last soup bowl over and took her seat.

Sadie remembered a time before her parents split up, when her father was still at the table, even though he wasn't Jewish and never did figure out what Shabbat was all about. But even then, it was the same old Shabbat. "So we'll wait another minute, and if they don't come, we'll light the candles," Sadie's grandfather said, as he did each week. And just as her mother was reaching for the matches in their little silver box that Uncle Bernie brought back from Israel, the doorbell rang. Sadie jumped down and ran to the door.

Aunt Deb and Auntie Amrita were standing there, hand in hand, with Jonah and Jasmin their twins standing in front of them. Her aunts both leaned down to kiss her, one on each cheek. Just as they did every Shabbat. And the twins pushed past Sadie and ran into the house, yelling, "Grandpa, Grandpa!" just like they always did. Locking the door again, Sadie and her aunts headed back down the hallway to the kitchen, to see Grandpa Sam hugging the twins and pulling them up on his lap, as he did every week.

"I apologize," Aunt Deb said to her sister. "It was all my fault. We got tired of bringing the same old challah. So we decided to surprise everyone. But I forgot to preheat the oven when I got home from work. Which is why we're late."

Sadie almost said out loud, "You're always late," when her Auntie Amrita reached into the large white plastic container she was carrying, and with a flourish, pulled out a tall stack of dark brown flatbreads. "Fresh from the griddle, and aren't they beautiful?" Aunt Deb said.

"We helped make them!" the twins shouted in unison. But Sadie was very quiet.

"They're from a recipe for Shabbat chapattis that my grandmother brought with her from India to Israel," Amrita added.

"They look delicious," Grandpa Sam said, as Amrita put them in the center of the table on the challah plate, and then put the blue and white embroidered challah cover over them, the one that they used every week. "I can't wait to taste them," Uncle Bernie said.

"They look like the bread in that Indian restaurant Carlos and I used to go to every weekend . . . until right before he died."

"What's the matter, honey?" Sadie's mother asked her daughter, looking over the white candles, the salad and stringbeans, the steaming bowls of chicken soup with noodles swimming through them, over the challah cover that her mother Sadie had embroidered—who her own Sadie was named for—to the opposite end of the table where Sadie sat in her chair, her face contorted, holding back her tears. "Sadie, sweetheart, we all miss your Uncle Carlos."

"Mommy, I hate AIDS and I miss Uncle Carlos all the time. But it isn't that. I just don't want there to be chapattis. Even special Shabbat chapattis. I want us to have plain old challah, like we do every week. And you, and me and Grandpa Sam and Ikuyo and Uncle Bernie and Aunt Deb and Auntie Amrita and Jasmin and Jonah saying the blessings over the candles and the grape juice instead of wine, because Uncle Bernie is in recovery but we're not supposed to talk about it, and . . ."

For a moment everyone was silent. Then, one by one, they all began to laugh. Soon even Sadie was laughing. "I want Shabbat to be the same, Mommy. Just like I want it to always be the same when you read me a bedtime story."

So Sadie's mother Ruthie stood up to light the Sabbath candles and lead them in the blessing, just like she did at the beginning of every Shabbat. And Bernie stood up to lead them in the blessing over the grape juice, just like he did every Friday night. Then Deb and Amrita and the twins stood up to say the blessing over the chapattis, just like they did each week over a challah, now tearing off pieces of the steaming chapattis and passing them around the table.

And everyone really liked the Shabbat chapattis, even Sadie, who asked for another piece. Then another. And another.

5
The Secret Stories of Rosanna Ramer

MY FATHER'S MOTHER ROSANNA was born in Brooklyn in 1901. Heir to generations of women and men who were rabbis, she attended the Italian Rite Rabbinic College in Venice, California, where she met my grandfather Maxím, a cantorial student. They were ordained together, married soon after, and hired to serve a joint pulpit at Congregation Beth Leah back in Brooklyn.

My grandfather died when my father Jacobo, their only child, was in high school, but I remember my grandmother very well. Tall and strikingly handsome, she was the matriarch of our family and served Beth Leah as rabbi and rabbi emerita for over fifty years.

My father, a physician, met my mother Geralda at the symphony in 1949. They were married a year later, I was born a year after that, then Ricardo, Marcus, and Laura. We four grew up in Stone Village, Long Island, where Dad opened his medical practice and Mom, a concert pianist, taught and filled our house with glorious music.

Dad told us how fierce a mother Rosanna had been, but for the four of us kids, Rosanna (she wouldn't let us call her Grandma) was a loving mentor, not warm and cuddly like our mother's mother Sophia, but an inspiring figure who read to us, went over our homework with us, and was always encouraging us to do our best in school.

As I got older I discovered that my grandmother was a noted figure in the wider world, written about, quoted, and interviewed on the radio and television for her opinions on any news that concerned the Jewish community. The source of her fame was her study of the writings by and about Judith the Wise in the three Talmuds, one on the relationship between Christians and Jews during Third Temple times, and her magisterial study of pre-Holocaust Italian Rite Jewry in Europe, which won the National Jewish Book Award.

Rosanna retired when I was in high school. My parents invited her to move in with them, but she refused. With increasing frequency over the years I would take the train to Brooklyn, to visit her in her huge old apartment. It was strange to watch her slow decline, never mentally but physically. She went from being a tall proud woman to a tiny bird-like cartoon of her old self, with the same hawk's nose, the rest of her bent over. When I was leaving she would always say to me, "Andrea, you are the eldest child, the eldest daughter. Remember, when I die—everything will go to the archive at the college in Venice—except for this one little box," a small sealed carton that sat on the floor beside her vast desk.

Rosanna died when I was in college. Her funeral was held at Beth Leah. A long line of friends, students, colleagues, and congregants told stories about her acute mind, dense books, and penetrating eyes. We sat *shiva* in her apartment and when the week was over and our visitors had stopped coming, it was Mom who said, "Don't you think it's time for us to open Rosanna's box?"

As its known guardian, I brought it back from her study, put it in the middle of the table, tore off the tape, and raised the flaps. We all leaned close—Dad and Mom, Ricardo and his partner Yumi, with their baby Kimi asleep in her lap, and Laura and Marcus and his partner Pedro—as I opened the box to reveal a stack of manila file folders resting beneath a folded letter, typed on pale blue paper:

"To my wonderful son and daughter-in-law, and to my wonderful grandchildren, and your beloveds, and to my wonderful great grandchild, here is a little gift for you, from a secret part of my life. Don't panic! It's nothing to be afraid of. No illegitimate children or my prison record. Just a few stories that I've written over the years."

We were all in tears, for in those few words we could hear Rosanna's voice; not the frail thin voice of her later years but her deep rabbinic voice, which needed no microphone to fill a sanctuary. And we were amazed, for she was a voracious reader, and in her library were rows and rows of scholarly books and sacred texts—but not a single work of fiction. Laura pointed at me, laughing: "Now we know where you got it from, girl." I wondered out loud why Rosanna didn't say anything when I was in 10th grade and confided in her that I wanted to be a novelist, or why she didn't say anything when my stories began to be published some years later. Ricardo answered those questions: "Come on. Rosanna never like to talk about herself. But secretly loved it when other people did." We all laughed, and I went back to her letter.

"I started writing stories after I retired, with all of you in mind, thinking about your lives and wanting to entertain you. I began with a story that my grandmother told me, and went on from there. I played with short and long, with elements of the *Tankaz* and of our history that I hadn't explored in sermons. I played with different voices, like a visual artist who might work in oils, water colors, pastels, pen and ink. I played with ironic colors, and dark ones, with humorous ones, mystical ones, and I want you to know that I had a very good time."

"I have printed out a set of stories for each one of you, which you will find in the folders below. They're not suitable for publication, but I hope you'll find them engaging, these small portals into other worlds. And I hope that one or two of them will touch you, move you, the way that each one of you has touched and changed and moved me. Your loving and adoring Rosanna, who is so proud of you all."

We were all teary-eyed as I pulled out the top folder and began to read the first story. We sat for hours at her dining room table, the eight of us, taking turns reading. Stopping only when the baby woke up, when we needed to turn on the lights, or take a bathroom break. And we laughed. We cried, meeting for the first time a Rosanna we never knew. These stories are our family's Dead Sea Scrolls, our texts from the Cairo Genizah. And as is the case with all Jewish stories—we being a small tribe—the stories of one of us belong to all of us. They're better than anything that I myself have ever written. And now, as the hundredth anniversary of Rosanna's ordination approaches, my family and I have decided to share them with you, finding them immensely suitable for publication.

THE CENTER OF THE WORLD

Every year at Passover, at the end of our Seder, we all say these ancient words: "Next year in Jerusalem." And everyone knows that we say them because for us Jerusalem is the very center of the world, the place that we yearn for, the place that we always turn to in prayer. But my grandmother Chaya told me a secret when I twelve, the time when a girl comes of age in our tradition, while we were in the kitchen rolling out dough for noodles. She told me a secret and made me promise that someday, if I had a daughter or granddaughter myself, that I would tell her exactly what she told me. But a few things got in the way. So please pardon me if I am only just telling you now.

"You see," Chaya told me, as we sat at her kitchen table kneading dough for bread, "everyone thinks that Jerusalem is the holiest city in the world. And it was, once, a long long time ago. But many many years before you were born, an invading people came and destroyed the city, destroyed the beautiful temple that stood at the heart of it. Twice after that we rebuilt our holy temple, and twice again our enemies destroyed it, destroyed the golden temple that was the very living beating heart of our people. And when the temple was destroyed for the third time, God went into exile with us, wandering from land to land. She went to Egypt, to

Persia, and to Spain. She went to Italy and Ethiopia and India. She even crossed the Silk Road toward the rising sun and went all the way to China. But eventually She got tired of wandering, and of all places, She decided to settle in the very village that I was born in, not here in America but far away to the east, in Italy. And She stayed there for a very long long time. But then, after most of us had left that part of the world, to come to this new world, She got lonely. And She did what the rest of us had done. She crossed a big ocean for the first time, She crossed the Atlantic, wandered around a little bit, and then settled down in Brooklyn, where to the best of my knowledge, She's remained. Although in winters I think She goes down to Florida, like your Great Aunt Natalia, or maybe all the way to California, so that She can relax for a while in the nice warm sun, and look at the palm trees, their long green fronds fluttering in the Pacific breezes."

MIRIAM AND THE BLOCK

She wanted to be a poet. She knew that. From the way that she felt when she listened to the very first poem she'd ever heard, when her first grade teacher read it to the class. The poem made her spin around inside herself and smile. She loved that feeling, and she wanted to do that, make a poem, for herself and for others.

She knew it was hard to be a poet. Very hard. First you had to get your Poetic License. If you didn't have one, you weren't allowed to write poems, and the government only gave out fifty-two licenses each year. The test was long and very difficult. Not to mention how much it cost to take it. Her family was poor. But they always encouraged her, told her that she could do anything she wanted. Her teachers said she wasn't living up to her potential. That she could excel, if only she put her mind to it. But they didn't think she would.

So Miriam began to study, began to excel in her classes, making her parents proud and her teachers happy. When she wasn't studying, she read poems, all the poems that she could find, practically living in the public library. And, when she was done with her homework (and sometimes when she wasn't, in a secret notebook that she kept hidden under her mattress) Miriam would write poems. Poems about herself, about others; about trees and bees, about dreams and the weather. Most were terrible. She knew that. And she thought a few of them were good. But if you didn't have a license, it was illegal to write poems, so she could never show them to anyone to find out.

Finally, Miriam graduated from school. She was eligible to take the test. But she had to make enough money, so she got a job in a used bookstore, so that she could get at even more books of poems. And she met other people from time to time who had licenses, occasional customers. And sometimes a famous poet would come into the store, a poet whose work she had read. And Miriam would shyly thank them for their work, but never tell them that she too wrote poems, because she didn't have her license yet. And each night after work she would go home to her tiny room on the edge of town, and read and write over a bowl of soup and a loaf of bread. And she was happy. Reading and writing and studying for the test.

The test was very difficult:

1. What is the difference between a simile and a facsimile?

2. What is a metaphor for?

3. Tell us who your favorite poet is, quote from their work, tell us about a poet you do not like, quote from their work, and then compare the two, telling us why you like what you like and why you don't like what you don't like.

4. Write a sonnet on the subject of your choice, where each line has only one word in it.

5. Write a haiku about writing a haiku.

6. Compose a poem of any length in your mother tongue; then translate it into four of the eight official global languages, and write an essay on the nature of the poem and how it changes from language to language.

The judges were impressed by Miriam's poems and her answers. For a day or two after the notification came, she was ecstatic, and even more so two weeks later when her official License came in the mail, a large document with fancy script, suitable for framing, which she did. And although by law she could now write poems without hiding them, any way she wanted to, in any of the official languages, in any dialect, patois, pidgin or slang recognized by the world government, she was so overwhelmed that suddenly, now that she was free at last to do so—she found that she could not write at all. She found that she had nothing to say, although web sources from every part of the planet and from all three lunar colonies had solicited her for her work, within minutes of her receiving her license. No. Somehow, the shimmering line that ran from heart to brain to hands had silted up, or dried up like a spring in a season of drought, and all of her words had stopped flowing.

To get her words back, Miriam knew that she would have to do something far more difficult than passing a test. She would have to test her soul, have to battle with herself, struggling through forests and jungles, crossing dangerous swamps and fast rivers. Her sanity and her very life would be at stake, if she wanted to get to the Mountain that gives inspiration to all true poets.

Alone, a pack on her back, Miriam set out. The journey was long and difficult. At times she thought that she would fail, at other times she doubted that her body could hold out. But battling her doubts and fears, she grew nearer and nearer to the heart, to the living center of creative magic, closer and closer to the sacred place where people are almost like gods. The morning was clear. Two moons, one indigo and one pale blue, still drifted in the emerald sky. There had been fog the day before, but it cleared in the night, and Miriam woke to see it, radiant on the horizon—the Mountain of Inspiration.

Heart pounding, she ate her meal, rolled up her sleeping mat, and broke camp. By mid-afternoon she had made it to the foothills. Trembling as she walked, she could feel beneath her the feet of all the poets who had gone there before her. Miriam made camp at the first plateau. Having survived a broken arm she had to mend herself, attacked by wolves, her toes almost lost to frostbite, she slept well on the mountain. She kept climbing, day after day, till at last she reached the top.

The wind was fierce. Hawks circled above her. In the distance, bear, deer, and threlk, lumbered, leaped, and lambled. At the very summit, with the planet spread out below, Miriam knelt, letting the power of the mountain enter into all her cells. First one, then another, then four at one time—poems coursed through her mind and body. They were real poems, true poems, the kinds of poems that would make others tingle, who had not, could not, would not, ever make it to the heights as she had.

And just where she knelt, she saw it. A dark blue slab jutting out near the side of the path. And the little metal chisel that her parents gave her when she got her License—she slipped it out of her pack, and set to work.

Years later, when Miriam was famous, she would sit at her desk with that hunk of rock in her hands. Feeling the power in it, that power of ancient stone, cobalt blue, opaline, sparkling; the only rock on the planet with the power to awaken poems. And she would cradle it in her hands, her writer's block, the words of her four mountain poems chiseled into it, pressing it against her cheek, her ribs, her heart, like a new born child, ancient and wise. And her eyes would close. And the stone would do its magic. As her body rocked and swayed, and filled up once again—with the night-glowing words of another breathful poem.

THE TRIAL OF TRIALS

The requisite period of rehabilitation had done nothing to change him. So reported the therapists assigned to work with him. A second round was equally disappointing, as was a third. "No repentance. No remorse," his team of angelic therapists informed their supervisors. According to the laws of heaven, after three such rounds the accused is ordered to stand trial. His court appearance began in an orderly fashion. The defending and prosecuting angels gave their opening statements. Then, as is customary in heaven, the defendant had the opportunity to speak. Standing, a steely look in his eyes, Adolf Hitler turned to the Judge and said, "I have seen, down on Earth, how since my death my name has been used to stand for Evil itself, when men like Stalin and Mao, who were responsible for far more deaths than I was, are viewed as defective rather than demonic. And ultimately I say to You," and here he pointed directly at the Judge, his voice grown shrill, "that it's You who ought to be on trial, for creating a world in which a soul like mine could be born."

With that, the courtroom burst in a cacophony of voices, of thousands of angels rising to their seats, wings flapping madly. "A mockery. An outrage. Proof itself. There should be no trial, just sentencing, when his guilt is so apparent." Such shouts and cries went on and on, ignoring the repeated calls for silence, till at last the Judge ordered the courtroom cleared of all visitors and declared the trial would be sealed from that point on.

Finally, the Judge, the defending and prosecuting angels, a single recording angel, and Hitler himself, sat mutely in the vast, still, golden chamber. And, ever patient, sitting on a small rise, the Judge waited till the very last echoes faded from the room, till the shout and flutter of departing angels had faded. Then the Judge went on.

"Herr Hitler, rest assured that in spite of the unusual circumstances of your case, and the recent, unfortunate outbreak in this courtroom, that we shall not, as has been called for, grant a decision in these matters without a formal trial. And please be reminded that in spite of everything—and I am not oblivious to the merits of your argument—that I have given you all free will. And whatever My possible failings in your eyes, sir, it is you who are on trial today, for your actions on Earth. You sir, and not Me. You, sir, and no one else."

To those words from the Judge, Hitler had neither comment nor visible response. He remained sitting, stony cold, in the defendant's box.

The Judge turned to the defending angel, who rose, with dark purple wings pulled close against its back. "Your Honor, the defendant has, in a prior deposition, acknowledged his full involvement in all of the events that he's on trial for. This is an unusual action in a hearing such as this, and I would like to mention it, to his credit." The defending angel turned toward the blue-winged recording angel, as it entered those words on a long silver scroll. "And I have already submitted documents to the court proving the deprivation of my client's childhood, the abuse he endured, and its lasting effect on his mentation." The Judge nodded, thoughtfully, and the defending angel, turning back to its seat, let the court know, "I have nothing further to say at this moment."

The prosecuting angel stood and flared its large orange wings, with a sudden loud snap. Hitler jerked in his seat and then brought his body under control. Moving toward the Judge's stand the prosecuting angel said, "Your Honor, my worthy companion here would like us to believe that his client's admission of responsibility is worthy of mention, and that the abuse he endured ought to elicit from us compassion, and in some twisted way not just explain but excuse his heinous actions. But from my point of view, admission without any feeling of horror at the great crimes he committed, without even the slightest hint of regret, let alone repentance, is both a mockery of his innate humanity and a mockery of this court." Having said that, it paused.

Seated in silence, the Judge nodded to the prosecuting angel, who continued. "Your Honor, at this time I would like to enter into the records my evidence." The angel continued. "Mr. Hitler, rather than reiterate all the crimes that you have been charged with, which are common knowledge in heaven and down below, I have chosen to approach this part of the trial from a different angle." Here it turned toward the defendant. "In a moment, in the air in front of you, a series of faces will appear, each one lasting for a single minute in Earth time. Each face will be that of another human victim of your heinous regime. These victims, men, women, and children, lost their lives not *because* you lived, but because of *how* you lived."

Hitler sneered, or so it seemed to the recording angel, as the prosecuting angel went on. "I have one further stipulation in entering this evidence into the proceedings, that you look at each face for the full minute that it's shown. If you fail to do so, the face will remain visible till such time as you have allowed it to register on your consciousness, the face, the very human face of a soul that was deprived of its chosen embodiment because of you. Let me remind you that there are 525,600 minutes in a standard Earth year. You can do the math, Mr. Hitler, if you want to know how long these faces will appear before you."

Here the defending angel rose and snapped out its own dark wings. "Your Honor, no one here will deny the crimes committed by my client, but we must not forget that he was himself the victim of horrifying neglect, abuse, violence, from the time of his birth."

"Many are wounded on Earth, my dear colleague," the prosecuting angel said, "but few turn into such monsters as your client."

"Your Honor, my worthy companion in this courtroom is making judgments about my client before this hearing is concluded."

The Judge nodded, "Your point is noted." And, given that Earth time is linear, and heaven time is fluid and expansive, let it suffice to say that Adolf Hitler's trial is still going on, in one of countless heavenly courtrooms, each presided over by the same One Judge. Alas, as it's a closed court, and since only the facts about the opening of the trial were released to the celestial press, I cannot tell you anything else about the proceedings, Mr. Hitler's response to the images, or tell you anything about how long his trial may last. Some say that, all this time later, Hitler is still looking at the very first image.

DEBRA LEIBOWITZ, ASTRONOMY MAJOR, IN TRANSIT

The room when empty is a perfect square, its walls painted white. Pine floor urethaned, an altar at the far end. Emotionless Buddha sits, massive, stony gray, carved. On the floor perfect rows of black padded squares. In the center of each, a round black cushion.

We enter. We bow. We sit. The silence is thick. A dense but electric energy fills the room. My back hurts. I begin to rock. The teacher, in black, wandering among us on our perfect rows of cushions, the lone electron orbiting, taps me gently on the right shoulder. In his home country, I know, he would slap me with a wooden switch. "Stop moving," his gesture says. He has told me this before, in words, in our private sessions. I told him my name means *Bee* in Hebrew, that I am always moving. Said with a smile. He didn't smile back.

I try to stop moving. I try to get it right. But the Jew in this body, wanderer, exile, cannot sit still for long. I try to use the Buddha for a mirror. But he is still, he is he, and my woman body is moving, moving, moving, cell by cell. Slowly I begin to sway again. Forward. Back. I think of the mantra we all learned in high school, that koan. Einstein's Psalm. $E=MC^2$. Then I try not to think of it. "Think of Nothing, Debra," I whisper in myself. Can't.

He comes again. Taps me again, then slides his lotus hand swiftly down my spine. I stop. I force myself to stop. I contain myself. I stop moving. On his next pass he touches me quickly on the back of my head. This touch whispers "Now you've got it right." And now the whole room, white walls, gray stone statue, row after row of us on our black black cushions, in our perfect rows, boxed like elements in the periodic chart, no, like the *names* of the elements in the periodic chart, sit stony still, eyes open just a slit. While beneath us, in the time we've been sitting, the planet has spun nearly 800 miles on its axis. And in its orbit, the planet has sailed over 67,000 miles around the sun. Swept up in it, Earth, sun, and all its planets, have soared more than 490,000 miles around the center of our galaxy. Just while we've been sitting. And our galaxy too has been racing, over 2,232,000 miles through space toward a celestial location known as the Great Attractor.

We bow. We stand. The square room empties out. And then the noisy subway, rattles me homeward, rocks me, rolls me. And I give myself up to it. Mass, in transit. The mass of me, in mass transit. All of me, all of mass, always, always, energy in motion.

And that night, on the pounding dance floor, I tell about it. Juliana of the dark eyes that sweep over my face, then blink, then shine back. Right hand is on my left hip. It slips away, grabs my left hand. Swings me away and then pulls me back, so close we're breathing on each other's faces. "This is prayer, Deb. This is meditation." Her lips on the conch of my ear, wet, on top of the insistent music. And the room is spinning. Just like it should. And she spins me out again, then pulls me back, my great attractor.

THE CHIEF RABBI

There are Jews all over the world, in the usual places like Los Angeles, New York, and Israel, in unexpected places like Yemen, not so far from our ancient home in the Middle East, and in unlikely places like Ethiopia and India and even in far off China. So why, I ask you, why shouldn't there be Jews in Hell? And if there are Jews there are bound to be rabbis, and if there are rabbis, in a place as big as Hell, wouldn't you expect there to be a chief rabbi, like they have in England, or Israel, where they even have three of them, Syrian, Italian, and Egyptian? No, you shouldn't be surprised that there's a chief rabbi in Hell, but you might be a bit surprised by who he is. (Yes, things change very slowly in Hell, and the chief rabbi is still a man, although when his term is over, in 300 more years, there is much speculation that the next chief rabbi will be a woman.)

The Very Right Reverend Chief Rabbi, (such is the proper term of address for him,) Binyamin Herzl, comes from a long line of distinguished Jews, and his own service to the Jewish community while he was alive was even more distinguished. He was handpicked to be chief rabbi by the ruler of Hell, Asmodeus, after the long and successful tenure of his predecessor, Shabbetai Zevi, the last man whose life work divided our people as we haven't been divided since the days of Rehoboam and Jeroboam.

"What is the role of the chief rabbi of Hell?" you rightly ask. My answer: to assist in the spiritual lives of his constituents, as they move through what used to be called punishment and is now called rehabilitation. Naturally Jewish Hell is different from Buddhist Hell and Catholic Hell and the Hell of the atheists and the adjacent Hell of the skeptics and agnostics. Jewish Hell is not a permanent affair. There is no eternal damnation in Jewish Hell. Captives in other Hells, on finding out this truth, frequently sign up for conversion courses, but the conversion process in Hell is even more difficult than on Earth, and very few dead converts are admitted to our ranks. Given the added incentive in Jewish Hell to attain release from it, as you can imagine, even with inveterate sinners, religious attendance in Jewish Hell, percentage-wise, is higher than that of any other Hell with the exception of the Hell assigned to those who in life couldn't make up their minds what religion to belong to and end up going to several. Here too, the incentive is greater in death for those who are ambivalent more than those who were in life attached to a certain outlook. Many studies have been done by angelic sociologists on this population and the surprising benefits their temperaments provide them in Hell.

"But none of this," you are shouting, "tells me anything about the chief rabbi!" Don't think I'd forgotten! My own exclamation point is intended. So now you shout again, "But Binyamin Herzl, Theodore Herzl, was the father of Zionism, the founder of the movement that lead to the creation of the State of Israel, the salvation of Jews all over the world, especially after the Holocaust! And now you are telling us that not only is he in Hell, but that he is the chief rabbi of Hell! That's outrageous, that's twisted, sick, heretical, blasphemous, insulting to Jews all over the world. In fact, you must be some kind of twisted pawn of the Arabs, the Palestinians, or some self-hating Jew of the very worst kind. So sick that I'm going to put this story down before it pollutes me any more. Taking about Theodore Herzl like that!" To which I can only say, "Yes, that's the very same Mr. Herzl we're speaking of, the Chief Rabbi of Jewish Hell itself." And you raise your voice again, even more loudly, to say, "But Herzl wasn't a religious man. He was a secular leader of one of the greatest revival movements in Western History." To which we respond, "How do you think he ended up in Hell?"

Please stop shouting! No one gets to Hell but by their own actions. Yes, we know that millions of you revere the man, but remember that Herzl kept in his home a Christmas tree, Herzl chose to not have his sons circumcised, and his favorite music was written by noted composer Richard Wagner, whose music most of the Jews in the world abhor, along with Volkswagens—but not Mercedes-Benzes. Please also recall this little known fact—that before he created the Zionist movement Herzl went to Rome to try and convince the pope that he would bring all the world's Jews into the Roman faith if the pope could guarantee the end of anti-Semitism."

"But the land of Israel," you say . . . and we interrupt you. One of the grave sins of your Mr. Herzl was that he led so many Jews into idolatry, away from worshipping God to worshipping Israel. On Earth this may be forgiven, but not in heaven. Prayer, charity, and repentance may avert the harsh decree, as the rabbis of old taught us to say during the High Holiday rituals. And they are right. Prayer, charity, and repentance may avert the harsh decree—but it cannot be postponed forever.

THE BOOK OF ELIAS, OR: IN THE WATER AT BABYLON

Elias Nakamura, a doctoral student in archaeology who lives in Babylon, New York, was relaxing in a hot tub, after a long day at work. A single candle was burning on the sink, and a CD was playing softly: Bach's cell suites, his favorite music. Suddenly the small blue-tiled upstairs bathroom was filled with a nearly blinding white-gold light, and in the midst of the light a figure was standing, right in front of the bathroom door.

"Oh my God," Elias thought to himself, "I'm hallucinating, from chronic sleep deprivation." A sudden wave of self-disappointment swept through him, common to many who are struggling to finish their dissertations after working on them for almost nine years. Then he said to himself, "But I'm a scientist. I might as well continue to observe this." And he turned to the figure standing in the midst of the light.

The figure in the light came closer and said to him, "I am God, Elias, come to you today with a message for the world."

Elias hadn't meant to. No, that isn't quite right. Elias wished he hadn't (at least not out loud) burst into laughter, but he did. He began to laugh both at the strangeness of the situation, lying naked in a tub of hot water, and at the strangeness of being spoken to by an indistinct but none the less human figure, which was standing in the middle of his bathroom, in the midst of a light so nearly blinding that he couldn't tell if the figure was female or male, any more than he could from its loud, reverberating but equally ungendered voice. Elias was laughing out of fear, not fear of God, but from fear that he was going crazy. And what was even more crazy—was that the figure in the midst of the light, the one that claimed to be God, started laughing too. And soon both of them were laughing so hard that salty tears were streaming down Elias's cheeks, and falling like rain into the waters below. And each time that Elias tried to stop laughing (and he would, for a moment) the laugher coming from the figure in the light would get him started all over again. And in the midst of the light Elias could see that the tears that the figure in the midst of the light was shedding were sparkling, opalescent.

And then, all at once, they both became very quiet, and the figure in the light addressed him again, this time more formally. "I am God, Elias Yukio Wasserman Nakamura, come to you today with a message for the world."

Laughter was now the very furthest thing from Elias's mind. Fear was far from it, any fear of insanity. The light that filled the room had poured into him along with God's words, and that light, as it spread throughout his body and entered every cell, had miraculously melted away all of his doubts about Who was speaking to him.

"But why me?" Elias asked, sitting up in the tub. "I mean, I'm not religious in any way." God smiled at him. "I speak to everyone,

Elias, all the time. The interesting question would be, why are you hearing me?"

"That's easy. You don't show up in everyone's bathroom like this. If You did, You can bet that You'd have a lot more friends than You do now. But all of this is so weird. I feel like some kind of prophet from the Bible, only I've never really read it, except for a few stories the only year that I went to Hebrew School. And besides, I'm only half Jewish. But I guess You already know that."

God chuckled. "Elias, I have no religion myself. And as for the Jewish part, let me say that I was never that fond of Hebrew, if you must know the truth. And I'm glad that you can now talk about Me in non-gendered terms, beyond the male-female trap that Hebrew forces you into. But frankly, English doesn't go far enough for me. I'm particularly fond of Tagalog and other non-gendered languages, so consider taking them up. This is not a command. Just a suggestion. Commandments are your shtick, not Mine.

"Yeah. Sure. But why me? Why now? Why like this? I mean, I've wandered between genders my whole life, so that part is fine with me, but why show up looking like some kind of a person at all, standing in the middle of a pool of light? I never thought that You were an old man up in the sky, or an old woman for that matter—but I didn't think that You'd be anything like this, either."

God knew that Elias was a believer, and always had been, since he was little and used to walk with his mother by the water, and kick his feet in the incoming waves, feeling that everything around him, the sand, the seashells, the waves, the sky, the clouds, the little airplane high above trailing vapor behind it, and he himself, and his mother, and their joined hands, that everything that is is part of a greater endless Ocean. So, in answer to Elias's question, God moved a bit closer, leaned over the tub and said, "Do you have any trouble believing that I created the entire universe?" Elias shook his head from side to side. "Well, if you don't have trouble believing that I can do *that*, why do you have trouble thinking that I can do *this*?"

Elias shut his eyes and sank down into the water. There was a war going on in his mind. Part of him doubted that anything like this could ever happen, not just to him, but to anyone. And then there was another part of him, he realized, that did not *believe* that this was really happening. No, it didn't believe, it just *knew*, that somehow, for reasons entirely beyond him, the Creator of the universe had chosen to manifest Itself in the middle of a cloud of light, right there in his bathroom. The moment his mind fully accepted that as the truth, Elias remembered that he was naked. He wanted to slide even further down into the water, but that seemed absurd. The water was clear, and even if he'd put bubble bath in, as he sometimes liked to do, and loved to do when he was little and still Eliana to his family, this was God he was trying to hide from. And besides, he realized, the figure in the middle of the light seemed to be naked too, even though he still couldn't tell what gender It was, so why should he feel embarrassed?

Stretching out in the tub, now quite at ease with what was happening, Elias looked up at God and said, "Hey, didn't You come here to tell me something?"

God laughed again, and even though he didn't know why, Elias started to laugh again too. And they both laughed, another good long body-blessing laugh. Then God leaned very close, and whispered in Elias's right ear, "I already have!"

Then It was gone, just as suddenly as It had appeared. The light, however, lingered for a while, dancing through Bach's stately notes, illuminating every blue tile, his green towels, soap, chrome faucets, potted fern on the windowsill, and the map-of-the-world shower curtain, pushed back. Then the light faded, leaving Elias in the tub, exactly as he had been ten minutes before, exactly the same, and at the same time, completely different.

THE BOOK OF JOE

Joe Abrams had the skill of a baseball player in training, the brains of a future doctor or lawyer, not to mention his sandy blond hair and piercing blue eyes, any one of which would have made a Jewish mother happy. And Florie, Joe's mother, was very very happy. Her baby, now starting high school, was the darling of their little corner of Brooklyn. His sisters Rosalie and Adele adored him. In Max his father's eyes, Joe could do no wrong. There was however one small thing that troubled Florie and Max. Joe had been writing poems and stories for years and his teachers said he had great promise. "From writing you think to make a living?" his father, a tailor, said to him each time he brought it up. His mother would turn to stare out the kitchen window, as if she might catch a last glimpse of her cherished dreams, vanishing down Flatbush Avenue.

Although he was the best runner on the track team, what gave Joe his greatest pleasure was writing for the school's literary magazine. During an editorial meeting in his junior year he met Sylvia Maimon an aspiring poet a year younger, whose family lived in a big white house with green shutters on the other side of the park. Sylvia was as dark as Joe was light, as smart as he was smart, as beautiful, talented, and well liked. She believed in Joe and over time, sitting with Florie in her tiny kitchen, she convinced the older woman that Joe could make it as a writer. At night in bed, Florie would pass on Sylvia's words to Max, until he too began to think that his boy could be a somebody, an American Peretz or Sholom Aleichem.

Then Hitler got in the way of everyone's plans, the Japanese bombed Pearl Harbor, and as soon as he graduated Joe went off to fight. He kept Sylvia's picture in his wallet and wrote her every week, no matter where he was. He wrote his parents weekly too, letters his sisters would read to them at the kitchen table, for they never did learn to read English, except for subway signs.

Joe came back from Europe with a gold medal from Congress, took advantage of his GI benefits to go to Brooklyn College where he majored in English, which seemed the best preparation for someone who intended to be a writer. He graduated at the top of his class, gave the valedictory address, and two weeks later he and Sylvia were married. In the old county a father-in-law would have supported his new son-in-law while he continued his studies. A modern man with old world sensibilities, Solomon Maimon thought nothing of supporting Sylvia and Joe once the newlyweds settled into Sylvia's room in his large old house. Sylvia put aside her poems to go work for her father, and night and day you could hear the tap-tap-tap of Joe's typewriter. Several evening a week Sylvia and her family would gather in the den to listen to another one of Joe's enthralling tales. On Friday nights they would have Shabbos dinner with his parents, and with Syl beaming beside him, he would read his stories to a living room packed with neighbors and family.

Joe didn't sell his first story, or his ninth, but by year's end you could find Joe Abrams in print in several small magazines. Two years later he and Sylvia were able to afford a tiny apartment in Greenwich Village. Three years later, just before Martin was born, Sylvia stopped working and Joe sold his first novel.

1958 was a good year. Joe's second novel came out that spring, and he was working on a collection of stories. With help from her father, he and Sylvia bought a small house in Queens. "In the country," Florie called it, the first time she and Max came to visit. Martin was four, and Susie two. Both had Joe's coloring and Sylvia's dark eyes, two little towheads running around the house.

Sometimes, after the success of a first book, a writer finds himself stuck, competing against his own work, his own reputation. But Joe's second book was better than his first. "Abrams captures the sound of immigrant dreams, and weaves them together," one reviewer said, "in language that's pure Whitman, a Jewish Whitman." With reviews like that and sales like his new book was getting, with a new house, a beautiful family, Joe was on top of the world. He was heading home from a meeting in Manhattan with his agent Eli on a perfect spring night. Whistling as he came up from the subway, he ambled down the block, surprised that there were no lights on in the house. "Syl must have turned in early," he thought as he let himself in. Then he saw a folded note on the table by the door, from Sylvia. She'd left him, and taken the kids.

Eli, when he called him, sobbing, said that all women were bitches. (He'd just been through a bitter divorce.) Stan, his best friend from Brooklyn, sighed and said, "Maybe things got a little too good. And Somebody, you know who, doesn't like it when things get too good down here." As for Herb, Joe's buddy from the war, his advice was, "You'll get over it, Joey. We came back from Europe. A hell of a lot of guys didn't."

Overnight, everything changed. Not just the end of his family, for Sylvia wouldn't let him see the kids, but suddenly no one was buying his stories. Stan was sure that Sylvia's father, a man with multiple connections, had talked to his friends in the magazine business. And the sales of Joe's books dropped down to nothing. Eli told him that there was no room in America for a good writer, which's why so many went off to Paris before the war. Herb, the only one who'd talked to Sylvia after she left, never told Joe what she'd confided in him. That he was a self-absorbed monster who had no time for his wife, her own literary interests, or for his children, but only for his typewriter.

A year after Sylvia left him, Joe's father died of a sudden heart attack, and Florie followed a year later, from stomach cancer. Eli, Stan and Herb thought that Joe would crack up. Neither of Joe's sisters, married and still living in Brooklyn, would have anything to do with him after Florie died. He started drinking heavily, never stopped writing, and put his anger into an unpublished novel, "She Killed Me Twice." When Sylvia called to tell him she was about to remarry and her new husband wanted to adopt the kids, Joe agonized over it and decided, "I want what's best for them. Maybe this is it."

From drinking, Joe went downhill. Eli, Stan and Herb, all drinkers themselves, alternately tried to stop him and then called and agreed to meet him in their favorite bar. "Writers drink," they said, trading stories of Hemingway and Fitzgerald. But they worried about Joe. His drinking was destroying him. His writing got darker and darker.

Stan, who taught at City College, got Joe a job in the English department. His students loved him, with rumpled hair, sitting on the edge of his desk. But half the time he showed up late or didn't show up at all, and only lasted two semesters. Then Eli's brother-in-law Louie invited Joe to fly out to Hollywood to work for him as an editor. Eli thought a change of scenery would do Joe good. But he kept telling Louie what was wrong with all his scripts and how they ought to have been written. Finally, after calling him "A dirty, drunken, washed-up, lousy has-been," Louie fired him.

Joe's stories from those years were as bleak as his life. One cheap room after another. Selling encyclopedias door to door, doing check-out in a supermarket, washing cars. The sort of life Jews are not supposed to live, and the sort of stories about life that Jewish editors didn't want to publish and the Jewish public didn't want to read. The Nazis were behind us. Israel was new. It was a time of prosperity. We wanted to forget all of that. Philip Roth's shocking new stories of sex and depravity were different. But ordinary drunkenness, poverty, the loss of a family, was beyond the Pale, and after a few years of getting only rejections, even from the magazines that used to wait for another one of his stories, beg for another one of his stories, Joe stopped sending them out.

Then Joe developed a skin condition. His hands and face were covered with scaly sores, which only added to his reclusiveness. And yet somehow, amazingly, in spite of everything, Joe and his body got through the sixties and early seventies. Waking up in another dirty little rented room, he'd stare at the ceiling through bloodshot eyes and say, "Why? How?" Forcing himself to get up, to go to whatever job it was he'd found that month, that week, he'd drag himself back to his room to write. It's no surprise that in 1974 his house made of paper collapsed. A neighbor found him passed out in the hallway of their rooming house in a puddle of urine and called an ambulance. He was rushed to the VA Hospital, unconscious.

In their different ways, although years sometimes went by between seeing him, Eli, Stan, and Herb had all stayed in touch with Joe. Joe called Eli from the hospital when he was sobered up and recovering. Eli flew out to see him and offered to help out. Cleaning up Joe's rented room Eli came upon his stories. They were good. Very good. Eli called Stan and Herb and they both flew out to the coast to spend time with Joe. It took the three of them and a hospital social worker to talk him into going to his first AA meeting. He started going to a gym, eating better, and after a few months, even his skin condition began to clear up, on its own.

Without telling Joe, Eli sent his stories to Mallory Stone, an editor he knew in New York. She'd wondered what happened to Joe and wanted to see more. When Eli told Joe, he was pissed, amazed, and sure that Eli was teasing him. But Mallory signed him on, and lucky for Joe, times had changed and the stories he'd written in his dark drunken years were exactly what the public wanted. His new book, "Cirrhosis of the Heart," found for Joe the beginning of a wide, new, popular audience.

In Seattle for a book signing, Joe met Elise Kahn, who interviewed him for her radio talk show, which featured visiting writers. She asked incisive questions and he answered them, insightfully. Afterwards, Joe surprised himself by asking Elise out for coffee. And she, who always kept a professional distance from the people she interviewed, surprised herself by saying yes.

Although their relationship was carried on long distance, by the end of the year Joe and Elise knew they wanted to get married. And—they were terrified. Joe still felt raw from his divorce. Much younger than Joe, Elise had a marriage and another long-term relationship behind her. But she loved, trusted, and believed in Joe, and he believed in her. They hadn't planned on having children. Hannah was an accident. In his memoirs Joe said it was an act of God. Aaron was planned. So were the twins, Rachel and Reuben. Joe was there with Elise each time she gave birth, coaching her with her breathing, holding her hands. And in spite of his writing, his book and lecture tours, in spite of being (in his own words,) "an old man," he was there with his kids in a way that he hadn't been the first time. Was there with them whenever Elise was on the road, on assignment, for she'd continued with her career and was working for a network news show as a film critic.

People say that artists live tortured, self-destructive lives. Joe once described the middle of his life as "two pieces of good rye bread with some slaughtered animal in between, dripping with ketchup." But when we look over his life and work we might want to remember that those fifteen years of hell, that dead-meat time, were only a small part of a very long, happy, and very successful life.

Joe got a Pulitzer for "Tales of a Cranky Jewish Father," and went on to write three more best sellers. And while from time to time his name had been mentioned in connection with the Nobel Prize, Joe wrote in his memoir, "My wife, my kids, my life itself, were all the prizes that I ever needed. Everything else was matzah balls in the soup." An Oscar for the screenplay of his book "Uncle Nathan on the Moon," that comedy about an old man in a nursing home with Alzheimer's, was another extra.

In an interview with public television Joe was asked, "How do you see your second period of success?" His answer was, "As a gift from God." To which the interview responded, "If anyone else said that, I'd think he was bullshitting. But coming from you, I believe it." And when old age came calling, it was gentle and easy, with no loss of mental clarity. Joe continued to ride his exercise bike for two miles every day, and then did ten laps in the pool. "Not bad for a man in his seventies," he said to Elise, each time he climbed out of the water.

There was a time when no one talked about death. "Suddenly" let you know it was a heart attack. "After a long illness" meant cancer or later, AIDS. In some ways, for many of his stories are about dying and death, Joe helped to change that. He could write about death and make it funny, and although most of his characters die badly, from what he called "fast suicide," (guns, pills, gas,) or "slow suicide," (cigarettes, drink, despair,) Joe came to the end of his days on Earth at home, surrounded by family and friends.

Elise had a hospital bed set up for him in the living room, with its spectacular view of the Pacific, and hired a team of nurses to be there round the clock. For a week he drifted in and out of consciousness. The day he died was clear and sunny. Elise was there beside him. Reuben was doing research in Antarctica and didn't get back in time, but Hannah was there with her husband Todd, Aaron with his girlfriend Tanisha, and Rachel and her wife Rosa, with their newborn, Max.

On the mantle over the fireplace to Joe's right were a cluster of his awards. The wall to his left was lined with his books, in twenty-two languages. Like a patriarch of old, one by one, each member of his family came closer, so that Joe could kiss them on the forehead. A wordless blessing. Then he motioned to Elise, who by now could almost read his mind. She cranked the bed up higher so that he could look out at the water, and holding her hand, his family sitting all around him on the bed, without labor or struggle, Joe Abrams died.

More than a thousand people attended his funeral and even more came to a subsequent memorial in New York. Stan, the last surviving of his friends, summed up his life this way. "He had everything. It was taken away. He got it back, multiplied." But three months later his editor Mallory Stone was going over Joe's notes for his unfinished novel, "Rabbi Susan's Third Gentile Husband." Wondering if Joe might have left some indications of where he was going with the book, she asked Elise if she could see the final volume of his journal, which was still sitting on his desk. Elise FedExed it to her, and when Mallory opened it she discovered, slipped in as a book mark, a handwritten note folded in half that read, "Call lawyer. Have him look for Sylvia and kids."

RABBI DA SILVA'S DREAM

Jennifer Greenberg and Deborah Sassoon went to see Rabbi Miriam Da Silva with a question: "Rabbi, our daughters Rachel and Leah want us to get a Christmas tree. We kept telling them that we're Jewish and they keep reminding us that they are too, but that a tree is a pagan symbol and has nothing to do with being Christian. What can we tell them? What should we do?"

The rabbi thought for some time. She remembered all the injunctions against sacred trees in the Bible, trees that were dedicated to or even represented the goddess Asherah. She wondered if some of her congregants had past lives in which they worshipped the Goddess in Her sacred groves, while others had served a male God and carried their anger about trees with them from Biblical times. Then she turned her thoughts to Purim, whose heroes, Mordechai and Esther, are clearly taken from the Mesopotamian deities Marduk and Ishtar. And she thought about that most seemingly sacred, even quintessentially Jewish ceremony, the Seder, and how it had been borrowed from the ancient Greeks, who held a banquet around a discussion topic, as we still can read about in Plato's *Symposium*. But in the end she could think of no way to integrate a tree, which so many of her congregants have in their homes and jokingly call "a Chanukah bush," into the fabric of the Jewish calendar year.

Deborah and Jennifer sat waiting for the rabbi's response to their question. The rabbi was silent for a long time, sitting with her eyes closed. Finally, she opened them and said, "I need more time to think about this. I'll email you in a few days."

Three nights later the rabbi had a dream. In the dream a fiery angel of God came to her and said, "Miriam. Miriam. Remember when Moses saw a bush all aflame. It was in winter when he saw it, near to the Solstice. And this tree that Rachel and Leah want, it can be a symbol of the burning bush that Moses saw. Tell them that. Tell them that their tree will commemorate a sacred time, but that it must be grown for just such a purpose, and it must be mulched or recycled at the end of the season. They may not cut down a tree in the woods, or it will not be eco-kosher. Tell them that their tree must not be taller than the tallest person in their family. Also tell them that they must never wear shoes around their tree. Every day that it's up they must sit near it and read and discuss the passage in *Exodus* about Moses and the burning bush. They may decorate it with colored lights but not tinsel, even if it's biodegradable. And if they hang balls on it they must only have ten, and never more, to remind them of the Ten Commandments and the ten mystical spheres on the Kabbalistic tree of life. And the decorations they hang on the tree must not violate the second commandment. But if they so desire they may place one single angel on top, to commemorate the angel that appeared to Moses in the flames. Tell them that if they do all these things, in just this way, that their tree will be kosher and a sacred reminder of the Presence of God in the world and in nature, which must be honored and preserved for it is God's holy creation."

In the morning when the rabbi awoke, she wrote down her dream and emailed it as an attachment to Deborah and Jennifer. They passed it on to their daughters Rachel and Leah, who were very happy.

AND IN CONCLUSION

Noted author and cultural historian Harry Da Costa Cohen, writing to his colleagues in the Resistance, after escaping from the Nazi death facility outside Somerset, Pennsylvania, described the "tenacity of evil" he witnessed. A week later, as I'm sure you know, he was recaptured, tortured, and killed. His account of the gleaming white facility haunted me when I read it—so different from what we all knew of the death camps in Europe—Auschwitz, Bergen Belsen, Buchenwald. Reading his description I imagined that the killers must been horrified by what they'd done there, and by what it had done to them—and after they defeated England in 1945, the Soviet Union in 1946, they crossed the Atlantic and created a slowly implemented but far more efficient final Final Solution.

First, of course, they had to defeat us, but their technological prowess exceeded ours. New York City went first. The pilot who flew over it, a handsome Bavarian educated at Oxford, as history teaches us, called it "Jew York City" when his crew dropped their atomic bomb on it. Washington DC went next, the following morning. Then Chicago, as we all know, followed by our surrender, a day later. We've all seen the pictures of decimated skylines, of victims burned, vaporized. I imagine that it was the vaporization that inspired Nazi scientists. They did not build work camps here, filled with the subhuman barracks we all heard about. Their labor camps were neat, well-run prisons, maintaining well-fed victims until it was their turn to be sent to the extermination centers. They did not duplicate the European gas chambers. Our skies and the skies of the former Soviet Union were not darkened by the effluence of crematoria, which required human attention, and attracted it. Instead they were replaced by immaculate white-tiled vaporizing chambers that instantly turned to dust the men, women, and children sealed inside. Nothing to be shoveled; no emaciated bodies, no charred remains. Nothing but dust and ashes, easily swept up or vacuumed, then added to the elegant moss-green compost bins placed on the edges of their large lush kitchen gardens.

I have been there, I have seen them, as a member of the Resistance, spying upon those camps, in Pennsylvania, Missouri, Wyoming, and Nevada. Who could have imagined it, in the early years of the last century, that the Nazis would target and exterminate over thirty million people they identified as Jews or having Jewish ancestry? A physical scientist could be in awe of the work they did, to crack the genetic code. We've all seen the iconic picture of Hitler, in the last decade of life, standing in the laboratory in Munich where Gunter Schmidt and his team discovered DNA and provided Hitler with the missing link in his quest to identify the Jewish vermin of the world. And we all saw on our new German color televisions in 1966, Hitler's esteemed successor Reinhard Heydrich announcing that the entire planet was now Judenrein, cleansed of all Jews. He declared the day, deliberately chosen, the 9th of Av according to the Jewish calendar, a global holiday. I remember the celebrations, on what for Jews has long been the saddest day of the year, the anniversary of the destruction of our ancient temples, and our expulsion from our golden home in Spain. Medals were given to all who had turned in Jewish neighbors, family, friends, along with bonuses and trust funds for their children's educations. I watched the festivities in an underground facility located in an abandoned silver mine in Nevada, where three of us Jews were in hiding, with a dozen other Resistance fighters. My proud Jewish colleagues Manny Schwartz and Sarah Cohen were captured and killed in a surveying action two years later.

Who could have imagined, a century ago, that the war to end all wars would finally be realized, in the mad mad dreams of a team of lunatics who accomplished what Alexander the Great could not do, what Genghis Khan dreamed of but did not succeed at, what Napoleon Bonaparte attempted but could not achieve—the defeat of his final ally, a rival emperor, whose surrender allowed one single man to control, for the very first time in all of human history—not just the known world—but the entire world. Tonight however the Third Reich's third Fuehrer can go to sleep knowing that he has accomplished just that. All of Planet Earth is his. And we know what you will do with it, now that you have destroyed the former ally you Nazis divided the world with. A monster in his own right, but never an anti-Semite, my bitter heart goes out to the poor last Emperor of Japan, who upon hearing a telephone threat to drop a hydrogen bomb on his island nation handed over all his lands and powers to Friedrich Kohler, Third Reich Fuehrer and Absolute World Leader the First.

And this is my last will and testament, written, as far as I or anyone else can tell, by the very last remaining Jew in the world. My colleagues in hiding and I have repeatedly scanned the computerized data posted after Kohler's announcement, of the genetic records of every single human being on this planet, and while I hope that others like me are in hiding, in their own secret underground arks, I rather doubt it. Those Nazis are so efficient. I shudder to think about the good they could have done with all of that efficiency. Poverty? Cancer? Mental illness? Birth defects? Premature death? And now new diseases, like the strange retrovirus that is threatening the world's people.

Alas, dear Friedrich's announcement was a bit premature. There was one little Jew who he overlooked, a feisty fearful Brooklyn Jewess, of whom there is very little to say. I joined the Resistance right after the conquest, and have been on the run for almost fifty years. If there is any triumph for me now—it is in knowing that Kohler and his Storm troopers will not defeat me, but the Angel of Death, who will soon be coming to get me, an old old woman, living in a windowless cave.

My accomplices have promised me that when I am gone from his dark dark world that they will send this letter to Kohler through secret channels:

Dear and beloved Fuehrer, I send to you very best wishes for a short short reign. And, my dear Friedrich the Powerful but not so very Great, I began by writing about my brother Harry, his Ph.D. in German Literature from Harvard no license for survival once North America was conquered, and I want to end with him. Harry is one of the best exemplars of a vanished people, and I am told that there is a display on his life and work in the brand new Pittsburg, Pennsylvania Museum of an Extinct Race, right across from one about his friend and colleague Susan Sontag. I hope that the next time you are in North America you will visit it, and think of me, this letter perhaps added to my brother's display. And in conclusion I want to assure you, dear great Leader, that while you have eliminated every last Jew in the world, a plague, the Black Death, a strange new illness, some unexpected scourge or assassin, a gigantic meteor from outer space, a massive volcanic eruption, an earthquake of a magnitude never experienced before in human history, will rise up and defeat you. And from the other side, I and millions of us will be cheering.

Sarah Da Costa Cohen
Underground, somewhere in Alaska
May 29, 2023

6
Riffing on Torah

THE TORAH BEGINS WITH two entirely different creation stories. One moves from chaos to order when God talks the world into existence and declares that everything It created is, "Very good," while the second story begins in an orderly fashion and ends with the painful expulsion of the first two human beings from the Garden of Eden.

I've been to Eden and been expelled, again and again, and since childhood what's brought me back to wholeness has been reading something by or about Judith the Wise. I did my junior year abroad at Hebrew University in Jerusalem, and one of my favorite classes was on the books of "Zichronot," gathered together under her guidance and direction. Our professor was a dynamic English rabbi whose lectures were further enhanced by her passion for printing out the texts we were studying on a range of vibrant colors. It was in Rabbi Myra Gordon's class that I read in depth two of the books of "Zichronot" that we skimmed through in Hebrew School, *Rachel the Dreamer,* on bright pink pages, and *Queen Helena* on blinding yellow. Hungry for more Judith, in a dusty bookstore in the New City I found a quintolingual version of the anthology of her stories that Rosanna had read to me from, this one with parallel rows of Hebrew, Greek, Aramaic, Latin, and English verses rising up on each page like a grove of sacred trees.

After reading about Judith, her family, the city she knew, and the monumental Third Temple that rose up in her time, I would wander off to the Old City, enter through one of the great triple gates in the massive stone walls of that perfect square Roman city, walk down broad cobbled streets lined with shops and houses, sit for a while in the great Forum, admiring the triumphal arches and broad avenues leading to the temple to Jupiter that became a church and then a mosque, wondering as all Jews do who walk there—"What was Jerusalem like in the days of Judith the Wise, and where were our three holy temples? Where were the hills and valleys we read about in the *Tankaz*, that our ancestors were forced to level, to create the vast flat plain upon which an entirely new city arose at the foot of the Mount of Olives?" And as a writer, walking through that marvelous square city, thronged with Jews and Arabs, Christians, Muslims, Baha'is, Hindus, Buddhists, Utarkians, Sikhs, and Zoroastrians, I'd wonder—"Where beneath my feet was the great library Judith founded, which historians tell us had the largest collection of books in the ancient world?" We know that all of Sappho was there, all of Aeschylus, in Hebrew and Aramaic translations as well as its original Greek. We know that there were whole texts from rabbis and scholars whose words survive in only a line or two in the Talmuds.

It was in Jerusalem that I came to love *Pirke Avot*, Chapters of the Fathers, Judith's favorite section of the *Mishnah*, compiled two hundred years before her time by her direct ancestor Judah the Prince. And I also fell in love with one of her many gifts to us, her own small text, *Pirke Imahot*, Chapters of the Mothers. While *Pirke Avot* looks back in time, in her own book Judith the Wise begins in the past and then steps out into our collective future. *Pirke Imahot* opens with quotations from Beruriah, Yalta, Ima Shalom, Julia the Elder, Rachel of Hebron, and other women scholars of early rabbinic times. After that, Judith the Wise offers us our first reference to a figure she named Tirzah, after the youngest daughter of Zelophechad in the Torah. Tirzah was one of five brave sisters who challenged Moses about the exclusion of women from the inheritance laws after their father's death. Tirzah was also the name of a city that was for a short time during the First Temple era the capital of the northern kingdom of Israel. It's referred to in *Song of Songs,* where the speaker compares his beloved to that city and to Jerusalem for their beauty. Rabbi Akiva called *Song of Songs* the Holy of Holies of our Holy Scriptures, and in Judith the Wise's deft hands, that woman and city are given a new life:

> What Moses began in the days of our liberation from slavery, Tirzah will seal for all times in the years of our eternal freedom. Each day when you bake bread, put a little bit aside for Tirzah, the anointed one, who will have traveled a great distance to get here, and will surely be quite hungry when she arrives.

Perhaps my favorite of all her verses is this one, which I can hear in the strong, loving voice of my beloved grandmother Rosanna:

> It is true that God may not be talking to you right now, but what is there to stop you from talking to Her?

In the spirit of Judith the Wise, I go back to the Torah of my childhood, the Torah of our history, the Torah of our lives, and talk to it, to Her, tell and retell stories, riffing on them like a jazz musician, the saxophone of my imagination wailing, sailing, chanting, sighing; blaming, singing, raging, crying; soaring, laughing, praising, dying, only to be born again.

WHAT I HEARD AT SINAI

We are taught that every Jew who ever was and ever will be was standing at Mount Sinai when the Torah was given. If you cannot remember being there, as I do, fear not—for the mountain remembers you.

I was standing to the southwest of Sinai, which was really a low rise on the edge of a small oasis. Moses had gathered us there to deliver a speech about our lives and our future, and we all assembled, the six hundred and twelve of us who had fled from

Egypt. I was seven months pregnant. When my baby arrived our number went up by one.

Moses, as I said earlier, was a short dark hairy man with a heavy lisp. When he was younger he was very shy about speaking, but as he got older he grew more bold. We know many of the things he said, on that day and others. His words were preserved in stories that were eventually written down, and then edited, but what so many people have forgotten is that everyone standing there heard God speaking, and we all heard something different.

Here is a verse of my Torah. A small short verse. When I stood at Sinai I heard God call out, "Love your neighbor as yourself," which everyone else heard too. I remember the day, remember that the cloudless sky was filled with light. And then She said, "Share your bed, your heart, your life with your beloved, that your days may be long on the face of the earth." But no one wrote those words down when I heard them, all those years ago, or they weren't preserved. But when I turned to my husband and took his hand, he must have heard the same words too, for he took my hand and raised it to his lips.

Then God said, "There are as many kinds of love in My world as there are trees in My forests and fish in My seas. There is parent love and child love, friend love, and that curious attraction we have to those we hate and fear, which is itself a strange kind of love. There is the love of a woman for a man, the love of a man for a man, the love of a woman for a woman, and the love of people who are neither men nor women, or are both And all of these loves, which may on the surface seem so different, are actually all the same. Then there is love of country, love of people, love of things and the making of things. There is love of places, and as the Maker of places let Me tell you that that kind of love is very important to remember. And finally, there is the love of a human heart for Me, which is the seed of all the other different kinds of loving."

I did not see anyone else write down what I heard at Sinai, as a few of the Levites were doing with Moses's words. But I've remembered what I heard that day in body after body. And finally now, all these years later, I am writing it down. I am writing it down for you and writing it down for our children, and for those who come after us. (If any do.)

PRIVATE NOTES TO GOD

One of my Hebrew School teachers taught us this midrash, that God said, "It is good" each time that It created something, because It had created other worlds before this one that hadn't turned out very well. Then It created our world, and everything turned out just right. But when I read the news, when I look around me, at the wars raging, and the deadly storms, when I think about the poisons in the air, the water, in our food, this is what I want to say to God: "You should have kept going!"

But here God stopped and here we are, on this beautiful dangerous planet that we have so damaged. As an inhabitant of this world, I thought it might be useful to send God some notes I've been compiling, from here on the front lines, in case It's too busy, distracted, or disinterested to be paying attention. Or, perhaps It's turned Its face from us, as the Torah says God sometimes does. Or, perhaps the problem is that God shaped us and breathed life into us to be Its partners, Its co-creators, then backed off to see what we would do. (I can hear the angels groaning, "Bad idea to have made them!") So if You haven't turned away, God, but are waiting for us to hold up our end of the deal, please consider these notes from one of Your colleagues down here, marked *Urgent*.

If You ever want to do anything like this again, I counsel You, please don't do it, at least not without some major design changes. And if there is any chance of You doing some renovating down here, the same items listed below will apply.

First, I'll start with something easy. I'm writing this at the end of a really bad cold. You probably don't know what it's like, but there's nothing worse than feeling a big wad of phlegm stuck in your chest and then spending the next four or five minutes bent over, red in the face, breathless, hacking away till that slippery greenish blob is dislocated and rises up, to be discarded, only to be soon replaced by an identical sibling. If You decide to make people again, and You decide that lungs are useful, and if You decide that getting sick has some purpose that's worth including in Your plans, please arrange it so that the lungs drain out through the feet and not the face, so that when we hack away everything drains out downwardly. Let gravity help out. You used it in so many other interesting ways.

On second thought, please reconsider illness. The lessons we learn from it, compassion, how to make chicken soup, are not good for the chickens and could probably be learned in other ways. Now that I mentioned it, the bladder and bowels ought to empty out through the feet too. It would make long car trips so much easier. We could keep a tin can or plastic bucket on the car floor and use it without having to use some filthy roadside rest stop. Maybe urine could come out of the bottom of the right foot and feces out the bottom of the left, or You could come up with something better, something that doesn't require us to use so much toilet paper, which is bad for the trees and bad for our water systems.

Speaking of bad, there's the subject of good and bad, and of free will. Some people say that we need bad to make us appreciate good, that we need duality to make us understand life, and that our choices in life are related to our capacity for free will. Well, if You really are God, the Eternal, Absolute, Omnipotent, Omniscient, Creator off all that is, was, and ever will be—it seems to me that You ought to be able to come up with a way for us to have free will without good and bad, without suffering and loss and pain. Pain from hacking up phlegm on one hand to watching your child be killed by a Nazi lunatic or a random bullet, aren't selling factors for incarnation.

Then there's the matter of death. Queer Jewish writer Gertrude Stein said that if we didn't have death, there wouldn't be room for everyone being born. Barring extended space travel—and wouldn't we miss everyone we knew and loved when they left?—death isn't the worst idea. It's just that it's often painful, badly timed, and emotionally disruptive. If ever You should create again a world like ours, please do something different with death. There could still be death, but instead of intense suffering and prolonged pain, perhaps it could come with advanced warning. Like, say, about three years before we die we'd start to grow spots on our back, in beautiful colors, that would gradually get darker and larger as the time approached. Then death wouldn't come as a surprise, we'd have time to get ready for our own death and for the deaths of those we love. It would come with spots, but with no suffering or pain, for the dying or for their loved ones. And perhaps at the end we could slowly fade out, like clouds disappearing. I think that would work very nicely. I'll leave it to You to work out the details, but You get the gist of what I'm trying to say. I'm glad to be alive. Earth is beautiful, even with all the awful things we've done to it. But please, no more earthquakes, floods, droughts, famines, or tornadoes. We'll all be very grateful. And if You like my suggestions and follow them, You can be assured of having more friends down here than You do right now.

Thank You for listening.

THE FORGOTTEN SAGES

We read in *Pirke Avot* these famous words that established an imaginary lineage for the rabbis of Judah the Prince's time:

> Moses received the Torah from Sinai and transmitted it to Joshua, Joshua to the elders, the elders to the prophets, and the prophets transmitted it to the men of the Great Assembly.

Two hundred years later, when Judith the Wise was looking back on her life and on the work of the convocation of sages who canonized the last section of the Hebrew Bible, she wrote:

> The men of the Great Assembly transmitted the Torah to the rabbis of the Solemn Assembly at Javneh, who transmitted it to the women and men of the Glorious Assembly in Jerusalem.

In her own short book, *Pirke Imahot,* Judith the Wise asked, reflecting on her ancestor's text—and I hear these words again in the voice of my grandmother Rosanna who first read them to me:

What about Shifra and Puah the midwives? What about Batya the daughter of Pharaoh? What about Miriam? What did she receive, and who did she transmit it to? What about Zipporah the wife of Moses, and what about all the other women of the generation of the Exodus and the years of our wandering in the wilderness? What did they receive, and who did they pass it on to? To their daughters, while they were kneading scant flour to bake into bread. While they were hauling water in skins or clay pots, up from nears-dry wells and tiny desert streams. And, in the middle of the night, nursing babies in their arms while the men were fast asleep, they sat around small flickering fires and told each other stories. And shared recipes, on how to cook lentils, how to heal a fever, how to make love.

I love those words, and go back to them again and again, the words of our fathers and the words of our mothers. But being the Gay Jewish storyteller that I am (or am I a Jewish Gay storyteller?) I can't help but ask—What about the people who didn't fit into any of those neat binary categories? What did they receive, and who did they pass it on to? In a 1973 interview with Allen Young, Buddhist Jewish (or was he Jewish Buddhist?) poet Allen Ginsberg said:

> Neal Cassidy, Dean Moriarity, who slept with Gavin Arthur, who slept with Edward Carpenter, who slept with Whitman. And I slept with Neal, so . . . So speaking from that line of transmission . . .

Who did you sleep with? Who transmitted their wisdom to you? Who have you shared it with? Have you wandered the borders and boundaries of gender, merging and changing and creating your own? Have you caressed your way into the deepest revelations of the flesh, in and out of bed, in and out of prayer, in and out of our tradition, because we are all made in the image of God, who is always breathing in and through us.

A FAITH OF THE EARTH

Moses received the Torah from Sinai.

 Why Moses? According to Rabbi Claudia the Elder in the Roman Talmud, it's because he was raised in the house of the daughter of Pharaoh, and not with his own people. To remind us that we can do the work of liberation without knowing anything about our people, and without knowing anything about our tradition, either.

Moses received the Torah from Sinai.

 The rabbis of old did not say, "Moses received the Torah from God," nor did they say, "Moses received the Torah from God at Sinai." They said that Moses received the Torah from a mountain. Why from a mountain, and not from God? Because ours is an ancient earth-based faith, its most sacred wisdom given to its prime teacher, from a mountain and through a mountain.
 Is this what the ancient rabbis were thinking? I doubt it. But like all good ancestors they left us their words as an inheritance, and we are free to do with it as we must, as we will.

Moses received the Torah from Sinai.

 From Mount Shasta, Mount Fuji, Mount Olympus, Mount Kilimanjaro, and Mount Everest, real name Chomolungma, "Goddess Mother of Mountains."
 Like all the sacred mountains in the world, our Moses received the Torah from a mountain, and inscribed the sacred words he received on two rocks, just as the Hopi and other peoples have inscribed their sacred truths on stones from the earth, to preserve them.

Moses received the Torah from Sinai.

From a mountain. By the ocean, listening to the waves crashing. Walking by a stream as it ambles over rocks. At night, looking up at the flaring stars. Whipped by wind swirling through the canyons of a city's streets. From a dog, barking joyfully as you come through the door. A purring cat curled up in your lap. Tenderly, from a lover. There we receive Torah. And then we pass it on.

THE LETTERS OF THE TEXT

It was late afternoon. Tirzah, the designated messiah for our planet, was sitting in her study, up in sixth heaven. The words of the Torah were floating in the air in front of her, their indigo blue letters shining out from a wide translucent silver scroll. But . . . she wasn't seeing them.

The light from the blazing firmament between sixth and seventh heavens was pouring in through tall windows, beaming long golden pens of light through the columns of her floating text. She looked up toward seventh heaven and might have lost herself in contemplation of God's radiant splendor—delaying her studies even further—but a tiny voice in her head reminded her that she had work to do. Coming back to the room, to her desk, to the great wide scroll unrolled and floating before her, she returned to the chapter she was reading, one of her favorites, only to close her eyes again a moment later.

Many years before she'd taken a seminar with Asi'Tam'Kah, a master teacher from the planet Quingi, on the role of individual scriptures after their messiah is dispatched, on worlds with multiple religious traditions. After class, by chance, perhaps, she happened to run into Moses and Judith, master teachers from her own designated planet, who were chatting in the hallway. They stopped to ask her how she was doing, then invited her to join them for lunch, and it's the conversation they had that day that was calling out to her from the past.

Tirzah, Moses, and Judith were sitting in a cafeteria on the four hundredth floor of the academy for messiahs, surrounded by students, instructors, and angels of almost every variety. She couldn't remember what they'd been eating or drinking, but she could remember the question she'd asked them, which was a follow-up to the class she'd just attended. A question about the role of the Torah after she'd been sent to Earth.

Tirzah expected Moses tell her about its deep roots, and Judith about how the Oral Torah rippled out like waves from the Written Torah, evolving and growing, and how it would continue to evolve and change when she was down on Earth. Instead, Moses turned to her across the glowing amber-bright floating table, and smiled a warm smile, which rose up a little higher on the right side than on the left. And he asked her two questions, one after the other.

"Would you please think about the blessing we Jews say to God for creating the world anew every day?"

Tirzah smiled herself, golden eyes twinkling, for that blessing was one of the very first things she'd been taught, eons ago, by her very first instructor after she was breathed into existence—his sister Miriam.

"Then," Moses went on, "would you please think about the midrash which says that all the Jews who ever were and ever will be were with me at Sinai?"

Tirzah knew at least a hundred versions of that midrash by heart, in many many different languages, all of which raced through her mind.

"And now, my dear," Judith chimed in, leaning across the table, the fire in her eyes diamond bright, "Will you please take one more step with us?"

Tirzah nodded.

"If the world is recreated by God each day, and if all the Jews in the world throughout time were with Moses at Sinai, can you embrace the possibility that Sinai is always happening, that Torah is always being given to us, over and over again, at every single moment of every single day? Not necessarily the Torah we continue to study, the Written Torah, and not the Oral Torah either. But a third Torah, a Torah of the Heart."

Eyes still closed, leaning back in her large blue overstuffed chair, Tirzah remembered how startled she'd been when Judith had asked her that third question. But then, a bright light had flashed in her head, and she'd said to Judith and Moses—sensing that this was a conversation they'd been planning to have with her for some time—"Yes, yes! I *can* consider that. In fact, that must be the reason I exist, the very reason that I'll be sent down to Earth some day—to remind everyone of that truth. And frankly, I hope that I am sent soon, because the people down there are really making a mess of it."

Smiling at that memory, Tirzah opened her eyes. The translucent silver scroll covered with indigo letters was still floating over her desk. Gazing through it and out the tall wide windows of her study, she could see hosts of angels rising up toward seventh heaven for their evening prayers. She rolled up and sent her silver Torah scroll floating back to the shelf behind her, where it joined the rest of the *Tankaz* and all of her other sacred texts, from every tradition on every single planet in this universe. And then she soared out the central window over her desk to join those shining angels.

THE END OF THE WORLD IS AT HAND

You didn't have to be in heaven to see that on poor little Planet Earth things were getting worse and worse. Animal extinctions continued at so fast a pace that scientists could not keep up with them, and even the so-called safe-haven "arks" all over the planet that had been created to preserve species began to fail at an increasingly rapidly rate. There was almost no grass left anywhere, almost no flowers, and very few bushes or trees left, except for the ones growing in the huge domed complexes that eventually covered the last of the arable land. So many insect and bird species died that there were children who had never seen a bird in flight, a butterfly flitting or a bee darting past from flower to flower. In fact, there were only a few old people left who could remember what it was like to go outside without wearing a bodysuit and an air-fix, the ironic name that everyone gave to their breathing masks, and only a few very old people still living who had actually seen a blue sky.

Radical climate change turned fertile lands into wastelands, jungles into deserts, frigid zones into steaming tropics. The polar icecaps melted much faster than scientists predicted, and thousands of cities and towns by oceans and rivers, places that had been inhabited for thousands of years, all had to be abandoned, including many of the most famous cities in the world. Poverty, hunger, old diseases and frightening new ones proliferated, in the old now domed still-habitable places and in all the new ones. Naturally, the human population of the world declined, radically.

The elites of every region created fortresses for themselves, some above and many below ground, but for the masses, large and small domed resettlement camps sprang up; densely crowded, crime-filled temporary homes that of course became permanent. And then an awful new disease came, that melted people's bones. It spread slowly around the world, but spread it did, killing millions of people in the first year. And just when scientists were making headway on finding, not a cure but a way to slow down the disease's progression, an even worse disease began to spread, one that killed all children who had not yet reached puberty. Not *some* children, but *all* of them. On every part of our already decimated world.

A sane person would have thought that that would stop the madness, but devastating grief only added to it. So wars—civil wars, race wars, gender wars, class wars—not only continued but increased, fought by people whose body-coverings made them look like medieval knights. There were wars over land, and more frequently there were wars fought over access to water, even to water that had long been polluted. And along with these more 'conventional' wars there a few small nuclear 'accidents'—including the destruction of Rome and Jerusalem and Mecca, along with most of Paris, Sydney, and a portion of the middle of what had once been the United States.

Desperate to avert the ongoing crisis on our planet, economic leaders came together, hoping to find a solution to the world's problems, but nothing they discussed and then implemented made even the slightest bit of difference. Religious leaders from every sect, cult, faith, denomination, tradition, practice, held endless prayer vigils, which did nothing, and tried to sit together, talk with each other, but that didn't work either. Political leaders, self-appointed, risen up from the masses, hereditary, elected, juntas, vigilantes, warlords, and peacemakers tried to meet, to discuss, to plan, in person and via the OuterNet, but nothing that they did did anything to improve the situation. Desperate, they tried new ways of connecting with each other. They meditated for hours, they did yoga for days. When that didn't work they tried smoking pot, took hallucinogens, drank beer, wine, gin, rum, vodka, sake, but none of that made a difference either. So they explored celibacy and when that didn't work they hired experienced sex workers to try to heal them, but that worked no better. Neuroscientists were summoned, who invented things for them to do and created new things for them to take, brain-altering medications that everyone in the world had high hopes for. But you cannot heal a planet with just with good intentions, any more than you can with good substances, and you cannot see your way to a better future when the past is screaming bloody murder at you.

In the midst of all that despair, people struggled to have "normal" lives, although "normal" was something from the past, something they read about in books and saw in movies, and heard stories about from their elders. One day Sarah Angela Gilman-Nakamura, a retired dancer and choreographer, had a dream. In the dream she was young again and dancing to a haunting melody that she knew was called "Naamah's Song." When she woke up, Sarah remembered the song. In happier years she had been famous for her performances, and famous for her fabulous parties. Knowing that she was moving toward death, and that life as she knew it on Planet Earth was also moving rapidly toward death, she decided to throw one last party.

Sarah found a venue, an old high school gymnasium in the heart of Brooklyn. Then she called her grandson Mechol'el Hassan-Leibowitz, who belonged to a band whose musicians came from every background, and she taught them "Naamah's Song." Sarah invited everyone she knew to her party. Having lived for most of her life in New York, and from having once been famous, she still knew several minor leaders in each of the seven leading global factions, and she invited all of them to her party. Desperate for a good time, all her friends and all the politicos came, leaving their outdoor air filtration masks at the door.

Sarah's friends all swirled and twirled around the large blue starry room, to the heartening beat of the Afro-Japanese-Palestinian-Hopi fusion band Mechol'el belonged to. At first of course all the politicos danced in their own little groups, with members of their own factions. But the music was splendid, with just the right beat, and soon a person from one group found themself dancing with someone from another group, and enjoying it. And lines of dancers began to form, snaking their way through the room. Then the band began to play "Naamah's Song." With ocarina, oud, koto, and drums, it spiraled like incense, like a delicate perfume, filling the room with its fragrance. And something happened to all those politicos from dancing that night, from dancing to that song. They found themselves not just liking but even loving each other—because they had seen and felt their very essential humanness.

Transformed by what had happened to them, several began deep friendships and others started love affairs. The minor politicos who were friends of Sarah decided to host a dance themselves, with the very same band, to which they would invite all of their senior politico friends. They decided to hold it in a dining room at the world government headquarters beside the East River, looking down on the rock garden where there were once beautiful rows of now-extinct cherry trees. And they hung a big banner across the room, which read: "The end of the world is at hand, but maybe feet can save it."

Most of the senior leaders of the world refused at first to attend, but they could see the hope on their junior colleagues' faces, and they found themselves willing to take chances that would not have made sense before. So they came, they all came. And they danced, they all danced. And then Mechol'el and the members of the band played "Naamah's Song," which they saved till nearly the end of the dance—and the world leaders found themselves weeping in each other's arms, laughing in each other's arms. Soon some of them were friends and others became lovers. And while that solved many of their personal problems, it didn't do anything to solve the problems of the world—but it gave the people of the world some hope again.

A NEW EDEN

Then something strange began to happen. And it happened everywhere, all at once, all over the world. The last of the scientists claimed that it was a mutation, but since most of their labs had been shut down due to the massive global depression, the only thing anyone could be certain of was that a strange new plant began to sprout—all over the planet. This new 'mutant tree,' as the scientists called it, seemed to be related to the fig, as it bore similar leaves, then flowers, and when the new tree fruited, the fruit it bore looked a lot like a fig, only rounder. But rather than being green or black—the new fruit of the new tree—had a beautiful indigo skin gently covering a pale beautiful aqua pulp.

On every continent, in every land, in abandoned lots and yards, on abandoned ranches and former farms, tiny shoots sprang up of this totally new tree. Because they were hardy they could grow in uncovered ground, with almost no water. They grew up in every climate, cold and hot, wet and dry. And in every town, city, nation, when people ate of the fruit, they discovered three things—one, that it was delicious—two, that just one fruit was a full and satisfying meal—and three, that eating one of those beautiful blue and aqua fruits made people happy and loving in a way that some of them had never been before, in a world grown sick and scary, where the average life expectancy had plunged to forty-five.

People were amazed that something new was growing, this new tree, sending up shoots and branches, then flowers and fruit. The seeds in the fruit were large and easy to sprout and plant. Soon these new trees were growing up not just in the wild but were being planted in yards, gardens, and farms. And soon all over the world, those broad-leafed trees were flourishing. And it turned out that those large beautiful emerald dark leaves sucked out bad things from the air. And it turned out that the roots of those new trees that people all over the world began to call "Ahuvah's Tree," it turned out that the roots of those new trees sucked out impurities in the soil, and when their dropped leaves were added to compost, they enriched it in ways that none of the former scientists could explain. And it turned out that there was an undetermined substance in those lovely aqua fruits that halted the bone-eating disease, and when fed to prepubescent children, kept them all alive.

When they ate even a single bite of the fruit of an Ahuvah Tree, the heads of nations and multinational organizations suddenly realized that what had been doing was wrong. And overnight, all around the world, all manufactured items that weren't 100% organic and biodegradable stopped being made. All genetically modified foods stopped being grown. People with vast incomes began to share the vast bulk of their wealth with others. Teachers' salaries were increased till they were amongst the most highly paid people on the planet. Stay-at-home parents were handsomely paid to stay home. Artists, musicians, writers, dancers, were subsidized because the governments of the world realized that in addition to plants and trees, that songs and stories must also flourish if a planet is to be healthy. And people who were at war for hundreds and thousands of years, made amends and made peace with each other.

Because all the people and animals who ate the fruit of Ahuvah's Tree became happy, and stayed happy, and generous, and openhearted, and respectful of everyone else, even if they only ate one small slice of one of those new blue fruits—the whole world changed, finally and completely, to become, finally and forever, just what we all knew that it could be, should be, all along. And the air got better, so that one by one towns and cities took down their domes. And within a decade, because of the way that Ahuvah's Trees pulled impurities out of the air, for the first time in their lives the remaining people of Earth were able to walk out beneath a golden sun without body suits or air-fixes, and gaze up into a clear blue sky. And birds began to come back, and bees. Lots of bees. And when people looked into each other's eyes, they all saw the same thing: love. Then the news began to report the same thing happening spontaneously, all over the world. Small groups of people—almost always four of them, because four is a holy number—at the breakfast table, in their office, a classroom, waiting in line, even walking down the street, would suddenly reach out hands, break into song, and start to dance with each other, at all hours of the night and day.

The angels said, "Finally."

God said, "Yes."

And that's when Tirzah the messiah came. A little bit too late. No, a lot too late. And right on time.

The End
or
The Beginning

Some things take place and are not true,
some things are true and never took place.

    Elie Wiesel

Whatever a disciple of the wise may propound by way of explaining law in the most distant future was already revealed to Moses on Mount Sinai.

    The Jerusalem Talmud

Afterword

Esteemed reader,

We have come to the end of our journey through *Torah Told Different*.

Andrew Ramer has opened doors of the heart to words and worlds of Torah that have been waiting for our discovery and exploration. We have been invited to sit with sages and seekers, prophets and dreamers, and as we have entered each of these enchanted lands they inhabit, we have been privileged to remember what has been forgotten. We have encountered Torah of motion and dance, Torah of music and songs of praise and pain, resounding shouts of joy and plaintive utterances of hope from all of God's creatures. In these pages, at least seventy faces of God, many never seen before, are revealed. How blessed are we!

When we Jews conclude reading or studying a sacred text, we acknowledge the mixed feelings of pleasure in our accomplishment and wistfulness that our rich and rewarding engagement with our sages has come to an end. We repeat ancient words that affirm our efforts and articulate our intention to return to the text to expand our understanding and deepen our delight. We say: May we go from strength to strength.

So it is with us as we conclude our reading of *Torah Told Different*. We have drawn strength from our travels through this magical land, and from our encounters with the extraordinary souls who have become our teachers and guides, challenging us, cajoling us, confounding us, delighting us. May we return to these

Afterword

stories, dreams, prophecies and parables and find Torah that was hidden in our first reading.

As we go forth, may we, like Andrew Ramer and Rachel the Dreamer, experience divinity as *Infinite Eternal Creativity*. This Source invites each of us to use the maps and signposts of *Torah Told Different* to see and hear and uncover new Torah, teaching that awaits each of us, every minute, every hour, every day, yet is too often unseen, unheard, hidden. This masterful work invites each of us to discover, dream, dance, and sing new Torah, new truth, revealing new sources of strength for living in our magnificent, complex, challenging, heartbreaking, beautiful world.

With gratitude to the Source of all creativity, the Source of all Torah, may we go from strength to strength.

Rabbi Sue Levi Elwell, PhD.
Scholar in Residence
Washington Hebrew Congregation

Notes

THE FEW "REAL" QUOTATIONS in this book from Jewish texts were translated by the author. All the rest slipped in from a parallel reality, as did most of the characters.

A TORAH OF OUR FOREMOTHERS

"Genesis Chapter Zero"—A slightly different version was originally written for Rabbi Elliot Kukla, in June 2009.

"The First Really Big Project," and "Emzara's Ark"—Noah's wife is nameless in the Torah, but she's called Naamah in rabbinic literature and I used that name in the first story. She's called Emzarah in *Jubilees,* written in the 2nd century BCE. Her son's wives names are shortened from the ones in that text. Lost to everyone but Ethiopian Jews and Christians who consider it canonical, many fragments of *Jubilees* were found among the Dead Sea Scrolls, indicating its importance to that community.

"The Life of Sarah" and the other Sarah stories are my response to the Torah portion of that name—which tell us of her death. They were also inspired by the following verses: *Genesis 24:1*—"The Eternal blessed Abraham with everything." In a commentary on that verse in *Bava Batra 16b* in the *Mishnah,* Rabbi Yehuda says that if Abraham had everything, he must have had a daughter as well as sons. The word *Imah* in the first story means Mother, Mommy, or Mom in Hebrew.

Notes

"With a Stranger"—I was tired of us being the people who wrestle with God, the meaning of Israel. I wanted us to live differently, with less struggle and more joy. Rabbi Tamara bat Zahavah offered me Jacob's new name, Mechol'el: "God forgives/a dance of God," which spiraled deep into my imagination and then outward through this book.

"ZICHRONOT"

One of the names for the Hebrew Bible is *Tanach*, an acronym formed from its three sections: *Torah, Neviim:* Prophets, and *Ketuvim:* Writings. *Tankaz*, the name for my four-section Bible adds a *Z* at the end for "Zichronot: Remembrances," which also shifts the sounds of the letters in Hebrew. It was created with the help of Rabbis Tamara bat Zahavah and Maurice Harris.

The following texts mentioned in the introduction to this section are "real"—*Judith, Tobit, Maccabees, The Wisdom of Solomon, The Wisdom of Ben Sirach*. There are actually four books of *Maccabees*. Read them all.

Rabbi Alberta Levy-Chan and the other rabbis cited in this section are fictional, except for Rabbi Irmgard Baum, named for my late second mother, who was not a rabbi, just an absolute marvel of a human being with rabbinic bearing.

Judith the Wise's words, "There are four things which guarantee that our people will endure," riffs on a line from *Pirke Avot*, "The world endures because of three things, Torah, divine service, and acts of loving-kindness."

Queen Helena was an historical figure; her companions in this section are not. An *etrog* or citron is a citrus fruit that is used during the festival of *Sukkot* or Tabernacles, held in one hand while holding a *lulav*, a cluster of a myrtle branch, a willow branch, and a palm branch in the other.

NOTES

THE FIVE BOOKS OF MOTION

"Sinai"—plays with elements of the story of Moses in the Torah, such as no one knowing where his grave is. It also plays with the statement of the great early rabbi, Akiva, who said of *Song of Songs*, the anthology of erotic poems found in the Hebrew Bible, that all Scripture is holy, but *Song of Songs* is the Holy of Holies.

"Alexandria"—Sometime in the mid-1980s I woke from a dream in which someone had discovered a few lost poems by Sappho in the ruins of Pompey, and published them. I woke up remembering a part of one of those poems and always wanted to use it somewhere. It's the first poem in this story. The others were dreamed by day.

"Cordoba"—The line about praying toward the east when our hearts are here, is a reversal of a line in a poem by Yehudah HaLevi, physician, poet, and philosopher, born in Spain around 1085, died around 1141, possibly in Jerusalem. He wrote that his heart was in the East, in Jerusalem, while he was in the West, in Spain.

"Jerusalem"—A *Ketubah* is a marriage contract. Some of the images here, such as being raised a princess in Israel are based on the words of a real person, Asnat Barzani, who was featured in an earlier version of the story. She was born in Kurdistan in 1590, educated by her rabbi father, who was the head of a yeshiva in Mosul, and married to one of his students, who succeeded him. At her husband's death Asnat, already teaching there, took over as head of the school, making her the first known woman to do so. I put elements of her life into the life of Judith the Wise, who I spliced into the lineage of the real Hillel and his descendants, including Judah the Prince.

"Sadie's Same Old Shabbat" was written for Rabbi Scott Slarskey, the only rabbi in the world to teach people how to chant Torah with a banjo, when the two of us were working at the San Francisco Jewish Community Center several years ago. He was looking for a kids story about Shabbat that had real people in it, people we knew.

NOTES

THE SECRET STORIES OF ROSANNA RAMER

Rosanna was invented. My father's name was Jacob, my mother's was Geraldine. I do have a brother Richard, who I sometimes call Ricardo. Marcus and Laura are named for dear friends I call my siblings, Marc Weinberger and Laura Paull. Everyone else is invented, whatever that means.

An early version of "Debra Leibowitz, Astronomy Major, in Transit," appeared on the website tattoohighway.org. When you meet Juliana in this story, I hope you will think about Emperor Julian, patron of the Third Temple.

"The Book of Elias: In the Water at Bablyon" An earlier version was written at the Winter Beit Midrash, taught by Rabbi Benay Lappe, in January 2004. It riffs on the first line of Psalm 137: "By the rivers of Babylon, there we sat and wept." (I love Don McLean's musical version, "By the waters of Babylon.")

"The Book of Joe" is a retelling of the Biblical book *Job*.

"And in Conclusion"—In addition to the obvious, I chose the name Sarah for the narrator to honor one of my mother's favorite performers, Sarah Vaughan.

RIFFING ON TORAH

Myra Gordon, my beloved aunt, was not a rabbi, loved reading Simone Weil, as did I, and counseled me to enjoy her ideas but not try to live as she had.

Please imagine and then write a 500-word essay on the Utarkian religion, its history, beliefs, and practices.

Pirke Avot, referenced in several stories in this section, is a real tractate in the real *Mishnah,* which begins with the line that I play with again and again, in different ways: "Moses received the Torah..."

Judith the Wise's invitation to put a little bit of bread aside for the messiah when she comes riffs on these words of Yochanan Ben Zakkai found in *Avot de Rabbi Natan:* "If you have a sapling in your hand, and someone says to you that the Messiah has come, stay and complete the planting, and then go out to greet the Messiah."

The quotation from an interview by Allen Young with Allen Ginsberg in 1973 was published in *Gay Sunshine Interview*, from Grey Fox Press, Bolinas, California, in 1974.

"The Letters of the Text"—An early version was written at the Winter Beit Midrash taught by Rabbi Benay Lappe, in January 2004. In an unpublished book, *The Music of the Spheres*, I wrote about a messiah named Rosetta, which is what I first called her here. Then I met Sue Levi Elwell, who credits *Queering the Text* with inspiring her midrash about Tirzah in *Chapters of the Heart*, which she co-edited with Nancy Fuchs Kreimer, also published by Wipf and Stock. (Read it. It's wonderful!) Inspired by Sue, I renamed my messiah Tirzah.

"A New Eden"—The very end, about Tirzah's arrival, plays with and diverges from this aphorism by Franz Kafka: "The messiah will come only when he is no longer necessary; he will come only on the day after his arrival; he will come, not on the last day, but on the very last."

Acknowledgements

These stories were shaped by countless books and multiple transmissions, for all of which I am deeply grateful.
Eden: Jayne Dworman.
Hebrew School: Miss Efros, Miss Heimowitz, Miss Stein, Mrs. Troyansky, Mr. Moskowitz, Mr. Troy, Rabbi Max J. Routtenberg, and Cantor Ben Belfer, at Temple B'nai Shalom, Rockville Centre, New York.
University: Houston Wood at Santa Barbara, Irene Eber at Hebrew University, Isaac Kikawada at Berkeley, for teaching me what and how to see, hear, feel, and read.
New York: Rabbi Lynn Gottlieb for opening the door to women's stories. Joan Larkin for opening the door to women's poetry.
San Francisco: My family at Congregation Sha'ar Zahav. My colleagues, friends, and students at the University of San Francisco. Rabbis Dev Noily, Camille Angel, Benay Lappe, Elliot Kukla, Reuben Zellman, Ari Lev Fornari, Julia Watts-Belser, Amichai Lau-Lavie. Cantor Sharon Bernstein, Penina Adelman, Aaron Hahn Tapper, Rose Katz, Randy Furash-Stewart. Pastor Sheri Hostetler and the First Mennonite Church. Jay Davidson for the home and even desk on which this book was written.
Somewhen: Bertram Brown, Steve Zipperstein, Cheryl Woodruff, for decades of sacred conversations. Rabbi Tamara Cohn Eskenazi and Rabbi Sue Levi Elwell for your words and your wisdom. Rabbi Maurice D. Harris for your close reading of this book and your superb doctoring of its pages. And Richard Ramer, always.

Acknowledgements

Everyone at Wipf and Stock, including James Stock, Matthew Wimer, Brian Palmer, and Shannon Carter.

The painting on the front cover, "Under the Sun," was done by San Francisco artist and gallery owner Anne Marguerite Herbst—www.anneherbst.com. The author's photograph on the back cover was taken by Shawn P. Calhoun.

This book was designed and typeset in Minion, a typeface created by Robert Slimbach for Adobe Systems in 1990. Slimbach was inspired by the elegant typefaces of late Renaissance. In traditional Jewish worship a Minyan is a quorum of ten adult men needed to hold a service, ten men and women now recognized in many communities. Both Minion and Minyan have their own rules of size, shape, form and feeling.

Andrew Ramer is the author of *Queering the Text: Biblical, Medieval, and Modern Jewish Stories*, and a co-author of the international best seller *Ask Your Angels*. His work can also be found in the following books: *Kosher Meat; Found Tribe; Love, Castro Street; Siddur Sha'ar Zahav, Jewish Men Pray*, and *Judaisms: A 21st Century Introduction to Jews and Jewish Identities*. The world's first ordained interfaith maggid (sacred storyteller), he teaches in the Swig Program in Jewish Studies and Social Justice at the University of San Francisco.

www.andrewramer.com

www.ingramcontent.com/pod-product-compliance
Lightning Source LLC
Chambersburg PA
CBHW050831160426
43192CB00010B/1981